UNDERSTANDING
OTHERS,
EDUCATING
OURSELVES

**Getting More from
International Comparative
Studies in Education**

Committee on a Framework and Long-term Research Agenda for
International Comparative Education Studies

Colette Chabbott and Emerson J. Elliott, Editors

Board on International Comparative Studies in Education
Board on Testing and Assessment
Center for Education
Division of Behavioral and Social Sciences and Education

NATIONAL RESEARCH COUNCIL
OF THE NATIONAL ACADEMIES

THE NATIONAL ACADEMIES PRESS
Washington, D.C.
www.nap.edu

THE NATIONAL ACADEMIES PRESS • 500 Fifth Street, N.W. • Washington, DC 20001

NOTICE: The project that is the subject of this report was approved by the Governing Board of the National Research Council, whose members are drawn from the councils of the National Academy of Sciences, the National Academy of Engineering, and the Institute of Medicine. The members of the committee responsible for the report were chosen for their special competences and with regard for appropriate balance.

This study was supported by Contract/Grant No. REC-9815157 between the National Academy of Sciences and the National Science Foundation and the U.S. Department of Education National Center for Education Statistics. Any opinions, findings, conclusions, or recommendations expressed in this publication are those of the author(s) and do not necessarily reflect the views of the organizations or agencies that provided support for the project.

International Standard Book Number 0-309-08855-0 (book)
International Standard Book Number 0-309-50640-9 (PDF)

Additional copies of this report are available from the National Academies Press, 500 Fifth Street, N.W., Lockbox 285, Washington, DC 20055; (800) 624-6242 or (202) 334-3313 (in the Washington metropolitan area); Internet, http://www.nap.edu

Printed in the United States of America

Suggested citation: National Research Council. (2003). *Understanding Others, Educating Ourselves: Getting More from International Comparative Studies in Education.* Committee on a Framework and Long-term Research Agenda for International Comparative Education Studies. C. Chabbott and E. J. Elliott, editors. Board on International Comparative Studies in Education, Board on Testing and Assessment, Center for Education, Division of Behavioral and Social Sciences and Education. Washington, DC: The National Academies Press.

THE NATIONAL ACADEMIES
Advisers to the Nation on Science, Engineering, and Medicine

The **National Academy of Sciences** is a private, nonprofit, self-perpetuating society of distinguished scholars engaged in scientific and engineering research, dedicated to the furtherance of science and technology and to their use for the general welfare. Upon the authority of the charter granted to it by the Congress in 1863, the Academy has a mandate that requires it to advise the federal government on scientific and technical matters. Dr. Bruce M. Alberts is president of the National Academy of Sciences.

The **National Academy of Engineering** was established in 1964, under the charter of the National Academy of Sciences, as a parallel organization of outstanding engineers. It is autonomous in its administration and in the selection of its members, sharing with the National Academy of Sciences the responsibility for advising the federal government. The National Academy of Engineering also sponsors engineering programs aimed at meeting national needs, encourages education and research, and recognizes the superior achievements of engineers. Dr. Wm. A. Wulf is president of the National Academy of Engineering.

The **Institute of Medicine** was established in 1970 by the National Academy of Sciences to secure the services of eminent members of appropriate professions in the examination of policy matters pertaining to the health of the public. The Institute acts under the responsibility given to the National Academy of Sciences by its congressional charter to be an adviser to the federal government and, upon its own initiative, to identify issues of medical care, research, and education. Dr. Harvey V. Fineberg is president of the Institute of Medicine.

The **National Research Council** was organized by the National Academy of Sciences in 1916 to associate the broad community of science and technology with the Academy's purposes of furthering knowledge and advising the federal government. Functioning in accordance with general policies determined by the Academy, the Council has become the principal operating agency of both the National Academy of Sciences and the National Academy of Engineering in providing services to the government, the public, and the scientific and engineering communities. The Council is administered jointly by both Academies and the Institute of Medicine. Dr. Bruce M. Alberts and Dr. Wm. A. Wulf are chair and vice chair, respectively, of the National Research Council

www.national-academies.org

Preface

Since 1988, the Board on International Comparative Studies in Education (BICSE) at the (U.S.) National Research Council of the National Academies has engaged in activities designed to increase the rigor and sophistication of international comparative studies in education by encouraging synergies between large and smaller scale international comparative education research, to identify gaps in the existing research base, and to assist in communicating results to policy makers and the public. Under the current grant (1998-2002), funded by the National Science Foundation and the U.S. Department of Education's National Center for Education Statistics, BICSE has sponsored public events and commissioned papers on the effects of the Trends in International Mathematics and Science Study (TIMSS), the power of video technology in international education research (National Research Council, 2001), international perspectives on teacher quality, and advances in the methodology of cross-national surveys of education achievement (National Research Council, 2002a).

This report responds to a request from the board's sponsors under the current grant to produce a report that builds on its previous work, particularly two earlier board reports: *A Framework and Principles for International Comparative Studies in Education* (National Research Council, 1990) and *A Collaborative Agenda for Improving International Comparative Studies in Education* (National Research Council, 1993). This report draws on the board's more than 14 years of experience in helping to strengthen U.S. participation in large-scale cross-national surveys of achievement and the collection of international comparative education statistics. The board's activities ranged from reports recommending ways to strengthen

UNESCO's role in gathering worldwide education statistics (National Research Council, 1995) to using TIMSS data to benchmark U.S. national education standards (National Research Council, 1997). In addition, the board has convened numerous workshops and seminars, including one on human resource needs in comparative education in 1996 and one on international research on teacher quality in 2000. Finally, as part of our work on this report, the board commissioned nine background papers to analyze the impact of different types of international studies and innovations on U.S. education during the 1990s.

This report has been reviewed in draft form by individuals chosen for their diverse perspectives and technical expertise, in accordance with procedures approved by the Report Review Committee of the National Research Council. The purpose of this independent review is to provide candid and critical comments that will assist the institution in making the published report as sound as possible and to ensure that the report meets institutional standards for objectivity, evidence, and responsiveness to the study charge. The review comments and draft manuscript remain confidential to protect the integrity of the deliberative process.

We thank the following individuals for their participation in the review of this report: Paul J. Black, School of Education, King's College, London, England; Kai-ming Cheng, Faculty of Education, University of Hong Kong and Harvard Graduate School of Education; Christopher T. Cross, Center on Education Policy and Education Commission of the States; Richard F. Elmore, Graduate School of Education, Harvard University; Steven J. Klees, Department of Education Policy and Leadership, University of Maryland; Barry McGaw, Directorate for Education, Organisation for Economic Co-operation and Development; Andrew C. Porter, Wisconsin Center for Education Research, University of Wisconsin–Madison; Francisco O. Ramirez, School of Education, Stanford University; and Iris C. Rotberg, Graduate School of Education and Human Development, George Washington University.

Although the reviewers listed above have provided many constructive comments and suggestions, they were not asked to endorse the conclusions or recommendations nor did they see the final draft of the report before its release. The review of this report was overseen by J. Myron Atkin, School of Education, Stanford University. Appointed by the National Research Council, he was responsible for making certain that an independent examination of this report was carried out in accordance with institutional procedures and that all review comments were carefully considered. Responsibility for the final content of this report rests entirely with the authoring committee and the institution.

This report in many ways reflects the accumulated wisdom of the board over the last 15 years and the committee is indebted to the 31 past members of the board who shared their time and thoughts so generously with the NRC. Special thanks go to Andrew Porter, chair of the Board on International Comparative Studies in Education from 1998 to 2001, without whom this report might never have been launched. His leadership was critical in holding the board's metaphorical feet to the fire, pressing us to address some of the more difficult issues we might otherwise have let slip away. His cogent arguments and pragmatism were recalled again and again as we struggled with those issues.

Special acknowledgments also go to members Clea Fernandez, Henry Heikkinen, and Lynn Paine. Clea Fernandez, whose perspective was so valuable in the infancy of this report, was excused in the later days to attend to her own infant. Despite recovering from an illness that prevented him from attending board meetings in 2002, Henry Heikkinen actively participated in the committee's deliberations from his home in Colorado and offered thorough comments on each successive draft of the report. Lynn Paine is also deserving of special thanks for her long service on the board, for bridging the "old" and "new" phases of the board, and for keeping us focused on the research that serves as the foundation for the board's work.

We appreciate Colette Chabbott, director of the board, who turned our ideas and sometimes rambling conversations into coherent narrative for this report. Patricia Morison, presently acting co-director of the Center for Education, provided much of the continuity for BICSE over the last 10 years. She has oriented and provided invaluable guidance to the last three directors, and under the current grant played a major role in helping the board expand and articulate its vision. Monica Ulewicz provided important research and writing for portions of the draft report, and Alix Beatty crafted solutions for revisions. Jane Phillips, senior project assistant for the board, shepherded the board through countless drafts with her quiet and efficient expertise. I wish to acknowledge staff of the Division of Behavioral and Social Sciences and Education reports office: Eugenia Grohman, for her guidance to the board in writing of the report; Christine McShane, for her editorial assistance with the final manuscript, and Kirsten Sampson Snyder for her guidance throughout the report review process.

We have been especially grateful to our sponsors at the National Science Foundation and U.S. Department of Education's National Center for Education Statistics—particularly Larry Suter, Jeanne Griffith, and Eugene Owen—who have, quite remarkably, represented their agencies in a collaborative relationship with the board over the course of 14 years. Finally, thanks go to Dorothy Gilford, the first staff director of the board

(1988-1995) and co-editor and editor of the first and second board reports; she helped us to think through many of the parallels and differences between the early years and the present as we prepared to write this report.

Emerson J. Elliott, *Chair*
Committee on a Framework and
Long-term Research Agenda for
International Comparative Education Studies

Contents

Executive Summary

The U.S. approach to education is not systematically informed by experiences with education in the rest of the world. Since the 1980s, many calls for domestic education reform have been justified by citing large gaps between the academic performance of U.S. students and their peers in other countries. Nonetheless, the U.S. public has been offered little evidence to explain these results and knows little about the limitations of the studies that produced them. Nor have U.S. policy makers and researchers used the limited information they do have about differences in education systems in various countries to systematically explore these results. This is surprising given both the ways that results of international comparative studies are so often used to justify domestic education reform and, even more, the ways that other sectors of U.S. society—such as business, science, and popular culture—have reached out to become more knowledgeable about practices in other countries. Furthermore, it is puzzling because the narrowness of many American's views of education is regularly noted, alternatives are actively sought, and criticism of domestic practices abounds.

In the past decade, federal funding for international comparative studies in education has increased and has begun to expand the knowledge base necessary to broaden the U.S. perspective. Most of this funding has been devoted to improving large-scale cross-national surveys and educational indicators. Nonetheless, to date this investment has not substantially raised the level of discourse in the education and policy-making community; most individual policy makers, practitioners, and parents in the United States know little more about education in other countries than that "we are not number one in mathematics and science."

Great obstacles prevent research, both domestic and international, from making an impact on U.S. education policy and practice. International research must also overcome a widely shared assumption that educational policy and practices in other areas of the world are simply not relevant to the United States. When we fail to examine variation across countries, we miss an opportunity to see and understand current educational practices against a richer array of options than those found in the United States.

Increasing the degree to which the wealth of education policy and practice experience across nations informs U.S. education policy and practice requires changes in U.S. investment strategies for education research. First, investments in international comparative studies of education need to comprise a larger portion of the overall U.S. education research portfolio. Second, within the international comparative portion of the portfolio, investments in large-scale comparative assessments need to be balanced with more investments in interpretive studies. Top priorities for new U.S. investments, principally in interpretive studies, include regions of the world and topics relatively neglected to date, such as Latin America, school governance, and school outcomes other than achievement. In addition, to complement this expanded investment and increased attention to interpretive studies, the board recommends

- routine consideration for including international components into major U.S. education research programs;
- support for studies using a wide range of rigorous and diverse research methodologies appropriate to the research questions under examination, including different combinations of those methodologies within one study;
- support for simultaneous primary analysis as well as secondary analysis and reanalysis of existing international datasets by individuals who are not involved in the collection of those datasets; and
- frequent production of syntheses of existing research findings on key policy topics across three or more countries.

Developing this more complex research portfolio will require long-term funding commitments as well as infrastructure to support leadership and coordination for a more systematic approach to international comparative studies of education. This leadership and coordination will serve as instruments to achieve the goals described above. More specifically, they will

- develop integrated oversight—independent from the conduct of individual studies—for major ongoing and proposed international research to encourage synergies across studies, to identify opportunities among studies for linkage and data analysis, and to bring attention to potential duplication;
- develop flexible criteria to evaluate and monitor studies that use different methodological approaches;
- ensure that new studies intended to produce datasets for secondary analysis include planning for that activity from the design stage onward;
- encourage greater participation by end-user groups in identifying and planning international comparative education studies and disseminating and interpreting research findings;
- plan better access to international and comparative education datasets and archives of primary source materials by both researchers and practitioners;
- use international comparative studies of education to stimulate national public dialogue on high-priority issues in education; and
- build up the international comparative education research community in the United States and other countries.

It takes time and effort to understand other country's education systems well enough to learn what they can tell us about ourselves. These systems are complex and interdependent; they can help us generate a host of new ideas but they are not blueprints for reform. The task remains for U.S. policy makers, practitioners, and the general public to test and adapt these ideas in ways that can improve education in America.

1

Introduction and Rationale

INTRODUCTION

The increasing scrutiny of earlier studies has revealed their limitations and the consequent need for improvement in the planning, execution, and dissemination of international comparative research.... The lack of an adequate system of education indicators to inform education policy making has become increasingly apparent. Data are not collected regularly, systematically, or with enough coordination either to satisfy natural curiosity about education systems around the world or to answer the questions of researchers and policy makers about changes over time in education in a variety of countries. Trend data are needed on many aspects of education.

A Collaborative Agenda for Improving International Comparative Studies in Education (National Research Council, 1993, hereafter the *1993 Agenda*)

By the last half of the 1990s, many concerns described in this excerpt from the *1993 Agenda* of the Board on International Comparative Studies in Education had been or were well on the way to being resolved. The proposed solutions, however, produced several new, somewhat overlapping problems. Previously, there was a scarcity of data sufficiently robust to support valid cross-national comparisons; today, a glut of good-quality data overwhelms the field and remains largely unanalyzed, even as new follow-on surveys are launched. Previously, large-scale cross-national education surveys were initiated sporadically, every few years; however, between 1999 and 2003, data collection for at least one and as many as three surveys was scheduled annually.

Previously, U.S. schools faced few mandated tests, and most were willing to participate in the occasional voluntary, internationally oriented tests; today, with increased requirements for mandatory testing, increasing numbers of schools are unwilling to add to their testing burden by participating in voluntary assessments. The infrastructure for conducting large-scale international studies that has developed over the past decade, which plays an important role in ensuring the quality of large-scale international education surveys, has become institutionalized, and the desire to keep this infrastructure engaged has played a role in decisions to support new and more frequent studies. Indeed, there is an increasing concern that international assessments are now conducted more frequently than reforms can produce change in the U.S. education system, which may discourage ongoing, longer term reform efforts.

In addition, the results of large-scale domestic and international surveys are raising a host of questions that often are addressed best by smaller scale studies requiring a wide range of research methods, both qualitative and quantitative. For example, although a full series of more detailed thematic analysis of the data was commissioned before the completion of the first Programme for International Assessment of Student Achievement (PISA)[1] international report, it was of necessity carried out by researchers closely aligned with the study. Few new initiatives have been launched either to cull insight from ongoing nonsurvey-based international studies or to support systematic new ones attuned to independent research agenda.

Despite major investments in a half-dozen large-scale international surveys over the past decade, U.S. public discourse about education remains curiously untouched by international comparisons. Beyond the common knowledge that U.S. students are not first in the world in mathematics and science, educational rhetoric in the United States remains essentially one-dimensional, lacking the sense of rich possibilities that international perspectives can provide. Possible reasons for this deficiency include the general imperviousness of U.S. education policy to domestic or international education research (Lagemann, 2000), and widely shared assumptions that other areas of the world are simply not relevant to the United States. The lack both of interpretive international comparative education studies and of secondary analysis focused on issues of primary concern to the public and policy makers, however, certainly contributes

---

[1]PISA is being conducted by the Organisation for Economic Co-operation and Development's Directorate for Education. It is a triennial survey of the knowledge and skills of 15-year-olds in the principal industrialized countries. It assesses how far students have acquired some of the knowledge and skills that the study considers essential for full participation in society. http://www.oecd.org.

to the persistence of an inwardly focused approach to education studies in the United States.

The Education Sciences Reform Act of 2002 places strong emphasis on using rigorous scientific methods to study education (U.S. Congress, 2002). This act has reorganized the U.S. Department of Education's Office of Educational Research and Improvement by creating the Institute of Education Sciences, which includes three centers: the National Center for Education Research, the National Center for Education Evaluation and Regional Assistance, and the National Center for Education Statistics (NCES), one of the main U.S. funders of international comparative education research. This is an important moment to examine the nature of international comparative education research and to reaffirm its critical contribution to a well-rounded program of domestic education research in the United States.

The purpose of this report—which is directed to federal sponsors of international comparative education research, domestic and international researchers, private foundations, and state and district officials who are eager to improve their part of the U.S. education system—is to lay out the rationale for such research; describe its scope, purpose, and potential impact; and make recommendations regarding future directions. Fundamentally, international comparative studies contribute to basic education research by documenting the existence of a much broader array of educational practices and outcomes than is available in the United States alone. International studies, however, can do much more than this. The rest of this chapter explores the current rationale for U.S. participation in international comparative studies and discusses the scope of such studies. Chapter 2 outlines the range of international comparative studies and their relative costs and presents recommendations for moving toward a more balanced research agenda for these studies. Chapter 3 draws on some recent studies to illustrate different ways that international comparative studies have—or, in some cases, have not—made an impact on the U.S. education system. Chapter 4 begins by offering suggestions for continuing to improve one type of study—large-scale, cross-national surveys—with which the board has been mainly involved since its inception, and to address key issues that persist or have emerged with those types of studies since the board's 1990 report, *A Framework and Principles for International Comparative Studies in Education* (National Research Council, 1990, hereafter referred to as the *1990 Framework*). It continues by addressing the pressing need for more public access to the findings of all types of international comparative studies and the consequent need for an array of studies addressing a wide range of questions that call for many different research methodologies. Chapter 5 examines the implications of recommendations from earlier chapters for supporting infrastructure, both financial and organizational, for future international comparative studies of education. The final chapter provides a summary of the board's recommendations.

RATIONALE

Although many features of international data collection in educational research have changed over the past decade, at least one has not: research that provides comparative information across nations continues to expand understanding of education as a social and economic institution and provide rich sources of ideas about how nations can strengthen teaching and student achievement. Throughout its history, the U.S. education system has benefited immensely from ideas borrowed and adapted from education systems in other countries. These ideas range from methods for early childhood education (France, Germany, and Italy), a model for the structure of higher education (Germany), and goals for mass urban education (England), to the Suzuki method of teaching music (Japan).

Holmes (1985) traces the earliest efforts to observe and learn from foreign education systems to Plato's reference to Sparta in *The Republic*. He dates the beginning of comparative education as a systematic study to the early 19th century. He mentions early reservations about the limitations of what is likely to be learned from such study. He cited one educator who claimed that "the practical value of studying other systems of education is that much can be learned about one's own system of education." His second claim was that "what goes on outside the schools matters even more than the things inside schools to an understanding of any system of education" (p. 866).

U.S. interest in international education studies has waxed and waned over the decades, but it grew particularly keen after the National Commission on Excellence in Education issued its report, *A Nation at Risk* (National Commission on Excellence in Education, 1983). That report made extensive use of findings from then-current national and international comparative studies of student achievement, portraying them in provocative terms.[2] The data cited in that report seized the interest of policy makers, who had little previous knowledge of or interest in comparative international education statistics but who subsequently evolved into strong proponents of comparative research at both state and cross-national lev-

---

[2]For example, "International comparisons of student achievement . . . reveal that on 19 academic tests American students were never first or second, and in comparison with other industrialized nations, were *last* seven times" (p.8).

els.[3] Some scholars, however, questioned the use of these particular international studies to judge the U.S. education system, given their imperfect sampling and other technical problems at that time.[4] Nonetheless, by 1990, the president and the governors acknowledged the importance of international perspectives in formulating domestic education policy when they defined national education goals for the nation. The United States was challenged to be first in the world in mathematics and science achievement by the turn of the century, and to ensure that every adult "will be literate and will possess the knowledge and skills necessary to compete in a global economy" (Rothman, 2002).

This focus on comparisons of achievement brought valuable attention to the potential benefits of learning about education in other countries. However, the country rankings that were so widely publicized did little to suggest the breadth of international research.

Cuban (1988) has argued that one remarkable feature of U.S. schools is how alike they are. In contrast, education systems in many other countries encompass a far greater degree of diversity. For example, there tends to be great diversity across nations regarding what citizens expect of their schools, what roles teachers play in society, and what education services governments and private organizations provide. International comparative research in education can help to expand the repertoire of possible practices and policies in several ways.

• International education studies help to *define what is achievable.* How much can students learn and at what age can they learn it? How do different countries mix different amounts of pre-service and in-service professional development for beginning teachers at the early childhood, primary, secondary, and tertiary levels? How do different countries determine the optimal number of hours of schooling at each of these levels? What roles do parents with different levels of education play in governing and supporting schools? Most people would be reluctant to conduct controlled experiments with their children's educations, but naturally oc-

---

[3]For example, a July 1994 NCES strategy document noted, "Education policy makers and analysts now routinely request information about how American schooling compares to that found in other countries . . . . The effort to provide a quality education to all of America's students has increasingly used international comparisons to assess our school's effectiveness and to generate ideas about ways to reform our schools" (U.S. Department of Education, National Center for Education Statistics, 1994:ii,1).

[4]For example, U.S. Department of Education, National Center for Education Statistics (1995:2) lists several follow-up activities addressing "the dubious quality of the data" in the studies cited in *A Nation at Risk* (National Commission on Excellence in Education, 1983).

curring variation in other countries can help develop more confidence in—or courage to consider changing—U.S. policies and practices. Studies such as PISA, for example, demonstrate that high average performance does not have to be associated with the wide disparities in performance found in the United States.

• International comparative research can help researchers and policy makers to *observe and characterize consequences of different practices and policies for different groups, under different circumstances.* Research can examine correlates of various approaches (Holmes, 1985; Postlethwaite, 1999) and explore the reasons for observed differences in student performance, thus enhancing confidence in the generalizability of studies (*1990 Framework*). It can also contribute to and possibly influence the content and direction of useful debate concerning public issues, such as teenage employment, and the terms of service of teaching, by enhancing the discourse through increasing knowledge about a wider range of alternatives and possible consequences.

• International comparative studies often *bring to light concepts for understanding education that have been overlooked* in the United States, helping U.S. educators to think in terms of new principles and categories. The Second International Mathematics Study helped to popularize the concept of the intended, implemented, and achieved curriculum and facilitated more nuanced discussions and studies about relationships between curriculum and student achievement. A recent book highlighting the expert, "profound" understanding characteristic of Chinese elementary mathematics teachers (Ma, 1999) casts new light on layers of understanding within subject matter knowledge. PISA's efforts to measure "preparedness for life" have led to new ways to operationalize different types of literacy.

• International comparisons of education often lead us to *identify and question beliefs and assumptions that are taken for granted.* This contribution is sometimes characterized as making the familiar strange and the strange familiar (Kluckhohn, 1944). International comparisons help to raise questions about the universality of particular features of the U.S. education system and offer new insight into current disputes. For example, Japanese teachers can offer cogent reasons why classes of fewer than 20 students are more difficult to teach than larger classes, and why, at the preschool level, teachers often should not discipline a misbehaving student.

Large-scale cross-national surveys have received much attention in the United States in the two decades since the release of *A Nation at Risk.* Many of the benefits of international comparative education studies, however, are achieved by relatively small-scale, low-cost, more open-ended studies. Such studies, in addition to contributing to our understanding of the broader range of possibilities in education, are essential precursors to large-scale studies because they help to identify contextual features of school systems that are common to many countries and can be quantitatively measured. Similarly, questions raised by counterintuitive findings of large-scale studies are often best explored by smaller scale, targeted studies.

International comparisons of education systems often produce outcomes that are not part of their original rationale but that nonetheless make valuable contributions to the improvement of U.S. education and international relations.

• In an increasingly interdependent world, they provide useful insights into the socioeconomic structure of other countries and cultures. For example, the insights of comparative education scholars who, in relative obscurity, had studied religious schools in Central and South Asia became more valued at the end of 2001, when graduates of those schools attacked the United States.

• The challenges posed by international studies can increase the educational research capacity of the United States as well as that of other countries (*1990 Framework*). For example, the Trends in International Mathematics and Science Study (TIMSS)[5] Videotape Classroom Study helped to raise the technical sophistication of video research methods in the United States and elsewhere. Furthermore, questions of sampling, instrument design, data gathering, and data analysis that had to be addressed in the second and third international mathematics studies yielded results and experience that have been useful in national surveys of achievement.

All these benefits do not flow automatically from every study. Rather, they are more likely to result from systematic investments in a variety of studies, differing in methodology, scope, and purpose, at least some of which try to test and build on earlier findings. Simply observing and measuring apparently effective practices in other countries is not sufficient to bring about desired improvement in U.S. schools. Ideally, promising practices would undergo several rounds of study in the context of their country of origin, and in the United States, in which practitioners and researchers attempt to construct and test hypotheses about the rela-

---

[5]The Third International Mathematics and Science Study (TIMSS) was conducted in 1995. Subsequent iterations of the same study changed the word "Third" to "Trends." Each iteration of the study is now referred to by the year it was conducted. Hence TIMSS becomes TIMSS 1995, TIMSS-R becomes TIMSS 1999, and TIMSS 2003 will remain TIMSS 2003.

tionship between the practice and desired outcomes in different settings. More often, informal experiments initiated by practitioners using innovations from other countries attract the attention of researchers post hoc; policy makers call on researchers to investigate promising practices; and, of course, researchers themselves may initiate exploratory studies. Instances of each of these cases are highlighted in boxes throughout the next chapter.

2

Range

Since the end of World War II, the U.S. government and private funders have supported a wide range of international education activities, including student and scholarly exchange activities in various disciplines, and the development of K-12 curricula to expand awareness and understanding of the rest of the world. By contrast, U.S. government funding for comparative social science research focusing on education in other countries—what we will refer to as international comparative studies in education—is a much more recent phenomenon, focusing to date on a relatively narrow range of studies.

This report redirects attention to the full range of international and comparative education studies. This range includes studies that involve one or many countries; collect large and small samples; employ a variety of quantitative and qualitative methodologies[1]; aim both to generate new hypotheses and test existing ones; and cover topics relevant to many levels, ranging from early childhood education to employment-related training for adults, and from governance issues for public and private schools to more practical issues, such as parent involvement in schools.

The breadth of these international comparative education studies and the way they spur interest in other research are illustrated by the summaries in the boxes scattered throughout this chapter. For the most part, these boxes highlight individual studies, rather than research programs

---

[1]For a more complete description of methodologies in international comparative education research see Rust et al. (1999:86-109).

or reviews of specific topics. For example, books and studies by researchers associated with predecessors of TIMSS 1995 fed grassroots practitioner interest in Japanese lesson study, a teacher-driven process of professional development. Lesson study experiments are now being conducted in the United States as action research, with small collaboratives of researchers and teachers from both Japan and the United States using ethnographic methods in a few schools and districts. These studies are partly hypothesis generating, partly hypothesis testing studies; at present they do not aim to make generalizations beyond the cases they are studying, although at some later point they may. In contrast, the data from Liping Ma's single-researcher study included interviews with only about 72 Chinese teachers, but Ma eventually used those data to articulate a kind of knowledge base for elementary mathematics teachers. Her work is now spurring domestic research in the United States on what Ma refers to as "the profound understanding of fundamental mathematics."

DIFFERENT PURPOSES

In this report, we distinguish three types of international comparative education studies according to their initial, primary purpose. Type I studies typically include large-scale surveys that aim to compare educational outcomes at various levels in two or more countries. Type II studies are designed to inform one or more particular U.S. education policies by studying specific topics relevant to those policies and their implementation in other countries. Type III studies are not designed to make direct comparisons between the United States and other countries in terms of specific policies or educational outcomes. Rather, they aim to further understanding of educational processes in different cultural and national contexts.

This typology avoids false dichotomies in educational research—large-scale versus small scale, qualitative versus quantitative—but it is not without difficulties. First, the domains of different study types are not mutually exclusive. TIMSS 1995, for example, was comprised of several somewhat independent studies, each using different methodologies. Some of these methodologies—such as case studies and videotaped classroom observations—are generally associated with more open-ended goals. However, all TIMSS components were undertaken to inform the overall goal of comparing achievement cross-nationally. The large-scale survey component of TIMSS is therefore an unambiguous Type I study. To the extent that the video study component of TIMSS was undertaken primarily to inform the survey, the video component is also a Type I study, but as a stand-alone study focusing on classroom interactions, it would be considered a Type III study.

Second, Type III includes the vast majority of international comparative studies in education, but Type I studies receive the vast majority of funding. Although cost is certainly not the most important factor distinguishing the three types of studies, it is certainly one of the most contentious and therefore figures prominently in the discussion below.

To summarize, the typology used here is based upon the initial, primary purpose, rather than the ultimate use of a study. The typology creates overlapping rather than mutually exclusive domains. Furthermore, the types do not neatly divide the corpus of international comparative education research into three equal parts, either in terms of number of studies or funding. This typology would be inadequate for the study of international comparative education research as a discipline per se. Rather, it is intended to expand the discussion begun in earlier reports (*1990 Framework* and *1993 Agenda*) to a broader range of studies and to a broader policy audience.

Type I: Comparing Cross-Nationally

Type I studies typically use survey data to compare outcomes—such as performance on standardized tests—in two or more countries. They also include rates-of-return analyses, social mobility studies, and many cross-national studies of comparative education development. Box 2-1 provides three examples of recent Type I studies. Many Type I studies to date have been large-scale quantitative studies with one of two primary goals. One goal is to monitor the status of a target population subgroup (such as 15-year-olds) in each country over time. These we refer to as indicator studies; the Programme for International Assessment of Student Assessment (PISA) of the Organisation for Economic Co-operation and Development is one example. The other goal is to understand the relations between education variables and to generate hypotheses about causal relations. Studies of this kind are referred to as research studies; of these, TIMSS is the best-known example and the Civic Education Study of the International Association for the Evaluation of Educational Achievement (IEA) is another (see Box 2-1). Although research studies of this kind may be very useful in testing hypotheses about correlations and generating hypotheses about the causes of these correlations, they are not well suited to evaluating causal hypotheses (National Research Council, 2002a).

Trend studies covering a stable group of countries can strengthen the grounds for speculating on causes but cannot establish them. As noted previously, the quality of both indicator and research studies has improved dramatically over the past decade. Nonetheless, areas for improvement remain. For example, these studies require continued efforts

Box 2-1   Comparing Cross-Nationally: Three Type I Studies

The *Programme for International Student Assessment* (PISA) of the Organisation for Economic Co-operation and Development (OECD) is designed to assess how well 15-year-old students apply and use what they have learned both inside school and outside it. PISA is the capstone of a large OECD education indicators program (INES). Fifteen is the age at which compulsory schooling ends in most countries, and PISA's outcome measure serves as an indicator of the quality of potential new entrants to a nation's workforce that can be compared cross-nationally. PISA surveys mathematics, reading, and scientific literacy every three years, with one domain as a primary focus in each cycle. In 2000, PISA assessed over 250,000 students in 32 countries (including 28 OECD member countries). A second round of the PISA 2000 survey was administered in 2002 to 13 non-OECD countries. PISA also administers student and principal background questionnaires to explore the social and economic context of the learning environment and students' attitudes toward learning. One of PISA's more interesting findings was that high average performance levels were associated with relative small gaps between the highest and lowest performing students in comparisons with the United States.

SOURCE: Organisation for Economic Co-operation and Development (2001).

The *Third International Mathematics and Science Study* (TIMSS 1995), conducted under the auspices of the International Association for the Evaluation of Educational Achievement (IEA) in 1995, assessed the mathematics and science achievement of a half-million students in over 40 countries at three age levels, which correspond roughly to the 4th and 8th grades and the last year of secondary school. TIMSS 1995 included several components: a curriculum analysis of 50 countries, a videotape study of 8th-grade mathematics classrooms in Germany, Japan, and the United States; a case study analysis of Germany, Japan, and the United States; and surveys of teachers and students to explore the context in which learning and teaching take place. The 4th- and 8th-grade cohorts achieved higher sampling standards than those achieved with earlier IEA studies.[*] The curriculum analysis related the mediocre performance of U.S. students to U.S. mathematics and science curricula, which it described as "a mile wide and an inch deep."

SOURCES: Peak et al. (2002); Schmidt, McKnight et al. (1997); Schmidt, Raizen et al. (1997); U.S. Department of Education, National Center for Education Statistics web site (http://www.nces.ed.gov/timss/); U.S. Department of Education, Office of Educational Research and Improvement (1998,1999); Wiseman and Baker (2002).

---

[*]The U.S. 12th-grade sample remains problematic for many reasons (Rotberg, 1998).

(continues)

Box 2-1   Continued

The *IEA Civic Education Study* examined school programs that promote civic knowledge, attitudes, and participation in more than 20 countries, in an effort to compare what young people around the world think about democracy. The study consisted of two phases that incorporated both qualitative and quantitative methods. In Phase I (1996-1999), 24 countries developed case studies to explore the context and meaning of civic education. Findings from these case studies then informed Phase II, an assessment of nearly 90,000 14-year-olds' civic knowledge and a survey of their civic engagement in Phase II. Phase II also included an assessment of upper secondary students to investigate the influence of additional years of schooling on students' civic knowledge as they approach the transition to adulthood. The assessment was an attempt to measure civic knowledge, skills in interpreting civic information, attitudes toward democratic institutions, and expectations regarding civic engagement as adults. The second phase of the study found that most 14-year-olds agree that good citizenship includes the obligation to vote. An area for secondary analysis is the gap between young students' perceptions about the importance of voting and low actual voting rates of young adults.

SOURCES: Amadeo et al. (2002); Steiner-Khamsi et al. (2002); Torney-Purta et al. (1999,2001).

to improve measurement of important school and student background variables pertaining to socioeconomic status and to experiment with cross-national comparisons using jurisdictions closest to the level of education decision making—such as school districts or states in the United States. Note that this last area for improvement is likely to increase cost by increasing the number of samples and observations. For example, in PISA, national samples of around 5,000 were required, but to make interstate comparisons, Canada tested around 35,000 and Germany around 80,000. Finally, those who conduct and sponsor these studies are still struggling to find ways to communicate the difference between correlations and causality in releasing their findings to the public, and to make clear that surveys are more often the beginning, not the end, of a research process that must involve many different types of studies.

Type I studies that collect primary data tend to be the most expensive, in terms of both direct costs, such as the diplomatic capital required to secure agreement at the national level for primary data collection and the cost of conducting surveys and employing experts to organize and direct them, and indirect costs, such as the time demands placed on student and administrator participants. But even within this subset of Type I studies, costs vary dramatically. For example, the estimated direct costs to the U.S. government of TIMSS 1995 are almost $20 million over five years. Other direct costs, however, including support for the Board on International Comparative Studies in Education (BICSE),[2] curriculum studies, and secondary analysis grants, totaled more than $3.5 million. In contrast, the U.S. contribution to the IEA Civic Education Study, much of it from private sources, was less than $1.7 million over three years.

The high cost of Type I studies must be weighed against the particular benefits. These studies enable us to establish benchmarks for comparing the performance of students in the United States to that of students in other countries. They also stimulate hypotheses about the reasons for differences in achievement levels in the United States and those elsewhere. The scale of Type I studies justifies spending significant sums on publishing and disseminating a variety of reports aimed at many levels of the education system. With help from public relations firms, these reports can attract the attention of a broad spectrum of the public and practitioners to specific issues in education, such as the depth of the curriculum. This is a double-edged sword: results issued with much public fanfare may dominate public debate long after smaller studies with much smaller budgets call them into question.

The relatively high cost of Type I studies increases the likelihood that attempts will be made to expand their potential uses by increasing the number of background variables selected, subgroups sampled, and topics studied, increasing cost at the design and data collection stages. As a result, two tightly focused Type I studies, each with a single purpose, may be less expensive than one expansive study, designed to serve many purposes.

Funding for the largest Type I studies derives principally from national governments and dwarfs funding for all other types. This focus on surveys is consistent with the pattern of development for federally funded domestic education research. The collection and dissemination of domestic education statistics was mandated almost 90 years before Congress authorized the U.S. Office of Education to fund broader education research (National Research Council, 1992).[3] Demand for Type I studies is often generated by policy makers. For the past 10 years, the U.S. Department of Education has worked from a draft multiyear strategy for U.S.

---

[2]This amount only covers the period 1992-1994, when BICSE's sole charge was "to support efforts to improve data collection of international studies of science and mathematics."

[3]Office of Education Reorganization Act, 1867.

participation in these studies (U.S. Department of Education, National Center for Education Statistics, 1994).

Nonetheless, the choices of timing, topics, frequency, and target group for these types of studies are not entirely within the control of U.S. policy makers, since the studies can be undertaken only with close cooperation from other participating countries. Sometimes U.S. participation in a study of relatively low priority for the United States may be necessary in order to secure broader cross-national participation in a study of higher priority. Every study that is rigorously conducted improves the capacity of the participating countries to produce better quality statistics, and in turn those can provide better, more consistent comparisons with U.S. education statistics. Conversely, by bearing more than its share of the cost, the United States sometimes persuades other countries to participate in studies of particular interest to the United States. For example, U.S. costs for TIMSS 1995 were very high, in part because the United States wanted more rigorous technical standards and shouldered much of the international costs of the study necessary to achieve those standards. The U.S. share of funding of both TIMSS 1999 and TIMSS 2003 were expected to decrease over time, as more countries adopt those standards and participate in cost sharing.

Type II: Informing Policy

Type II studies are designed to inform U.S. education policy in a direct way, by examining specific policies and their implementation in other countries. Type II studies also include evaluations of attempts in the United States to implement similar policies and practices originating in other countries. Many issues—for example, innovation and change, teacher involvement in change, and teacher development—simply cannot be addressed by Type I studies. Such studies demand a mix of quantitative and qualitative, descriptive and interpretive studies. A study of the experience of U.S. schools that have implemented the Singapore mathematics curriculum falls into this category, as do school choice and high school tracking studies (see Box 2-2) and many of the studies produced by the Organisation for Economic Co-operation and Development, such as the 13-nation study of educational innovation and change in science and mathematics education (Black and Atkin, 1996; Raizen and Britton, 1997). These studies may be initiated by policy makers or by researchers, either anticipating or responding to U.S. interest in specific policies or practices in other countries.

Type II studies tend to be smaller in scale and therefore less expensive than those Type I studies that collect primary data, although they may be more costly than Type III studies (described below). Studies that aim to

Box 2-2   Informing Policy: Three Type II Studies

Singapore Mathematics Curriculum Study. Singapore's mathematics curriculum has attracted attention in the United States because of Singapore's
high achievement results on international assessments. Approximately 100
U.S. schools have adopted Singapore's mathematics textbooks as part of their
reform efforts in mathematics education. The U.S. Department of Education
has funded a joint study with the Singapore Ministry of Education to assess the
implementation of the Singapore mathematics program in U.S. schools.

This 27-month study will include observations of Singapore classrooms
by U.S. district and school staff; site visits to U.S. schools using the
Singapore mathematics approach, including observations by Singapore
experts; surveys of district mathematics coordinators, principals, and teachers; and electronic networking among study participants.

SOURCE: U.S. Department of Education, Planning and Evaluation Services (2002).

School Vouchers. Private school vouchers are widely debated as a potential means of addressing the quality of the public education available to
some students in the United States, with proponents insisting that private
schools can deliver education more effectively at a lower cost and opponents arguing that vouchers take much-needed resources away from public
schools. To inform this debate, McEwan and Carnoy (2000) assessed the
relative effectiveness and efficiency of Chile's voucher system, which has
been implemented on a large scale and has prompted an increase in private school supply. The researchers defined effectiveness as higher academic achievement, holding student background constant, using data from
Chile's national assessment of mathematics and Spanish achievement.
They defined efficiency as producing the same achievement with less funding, using multiple data sources to construct a proxy of the annual per-
student cost of each school in 1996. Although not the first analysis of
Chile's public and private school achievement, this study used a more complete set of student achievement data, divided the voucher schools into
three categories rather than considering them as a whole, and provided the
only comprehensive analysis of costs and efficiency.

As the researchers point out, the findings from the study "are probably
not satisfying for either voucher advocates or opponents" (p. 227). Their
results suggest that nonreligious private schools are marginally less effective than public schools—even less effective when located outside
Santiago—but more efficient at producing achievement at a lower cost.
Catholic schools are more effective than public schools, but because of the
additional resources consumed in producing that achievement, are relatively similar in efficiency. McEwan and Carnoy draw inferences from
these findings for the U.S. debate on school choice. They suggest that the
United States may want to rethink existing comparisons of Catholic and

(continues)

Box 2-2   Continued

public schools as direct evidence of the potential impact of a large-scale voucher plan.

SOURCE: Adapted from McEwan and Carnoy (2000).

High School Tracking. Tracking, the controversial practice of assigning students to groups or classes for instruction based on their prior academic performance, has been extensively studied in the United States, but where international studies are available, they have interesting implications for U.S. findings. U.S. findings clearly demonstrate that achievement inequality between students assigned to different tracks (e.g. college preparatory versus vocational, or honors versus remedial classes) widens over time, but because almost all high schools are tracked, there is relatively little U.S. evidence on the effects of tracking versus the absence of tracking.

An important study of tracking in Britain by Alan C. Kerckhoff (1986) indicated that students in elite schools and high tracks gained from being placed in such educational settings, compared with similar students in comprehensive schools and mixed-ability classes. Meanwhile, students assigned to low-status schools and classes within schools fall further and further behind, compared with similar students in untracked schools and classes. Kerckhoff's results were based on a unique dataset consisting of all children born in England and Wales during the first week of March 1958 and provided compelling evidence for the effects of tracking on achievement inequality.

Many American studies of tracking follow students over time but lack evidence on changes in systems of tracking over time. Adam Gamoran (1996) examined four waves of survey data on high school students in Scotland during a time in which the secondary education system became less stratified (1984-1990), to determine whether the reduction in tracking led to lower levels of social inequality in educational outcomes. Not only were outcomes less unequal after the reform, but also achievement levels on a national examination were higher overall. This study showed that reducing tracking can lead to less inequality without harming achievement levels.

A third international study, this one comparing Israel and the United States, found that while schools with more intense tracking systems produce more inequality in the United States, that was not the case for Israel (Ayalon and Gamoran, 2000). A key difference between the United States and both Israel and Scotland is that the latter countries have national examinations that provide incentives for student performance in lower-level academic classes as well as for those in elite classes. On the basis of these results, one may speculate that the current emphasis on testing in American schools may lead to better performance among low achievers—if their teachers are well prepared, and if the students have adequate opportunities to learn the material on the tests.

SOURCES: Ayalon and Gamoran (2000); Gamoran (1996); Kerchoff (1986).

make inferences relative to policy at decentralized levels may require larger sample sizes for primary data collection than broader, more generalized studies. Type II studies, however, do not necessarily require primary data collection. Meta-analyses of existing datasets, or syntheses of existing studies across countries, are also valuable; both the *1990 Framework* and the *1993 Agenda* reports specifically encouraged the United States to participate in more of this type of research, in order to get the most out of existing studies. Like Type I studies, Type II studies must draw on a limited pool of experts; they also require modest diplomatic capital.

Neither the federal government nor states have established formal priorities or budgets for this type of study, although they offer the most direct means to explore causal links between public policies and the performance of the education system, often for a fraction of the cost of Type I studies.

Type III: Understanding Education Broadly

Type III studies are designed to increase general understanding about education systems and processes. Such studies are not designed to have immediate policy relevance, though many are of relevance to policy makers. Rather these studies are designed to bring to light new concepts, to stimulate interest in educational issues, to generally deepen understanding of education as a practice and as a social phenomenon and, most generally, to establish the foundation on which all other comparative education research is based.

These studies, like Type II studies, may be qualitative or quantitative, large- or small-scale, incorporating positivist, interpretive, or critical perspectives (Heck and Hallinger, 1999:143). However, unlike the other two types, Type III studies do not fall neatly under one purpose. Donmoyer (1999) identifies at least five potential purposes for qualitative Type III studies. These include efforts to answer the questions "What is the correct answer (assuming a particularly clear question)?" or "How do the people studied interpret the phenomenon?" or "How does an organization, individual, or group of individuals change over time?" or "How can the researchers simultaneously learn about and change educators and/or educational organizations?" Some quantitative Type III studies also relate to Donmoyer's purposes and others'. To designate all these studies as one type does not do them justice, yet to disaggregate them systematically is a task larger than the charge of this report.

As described in Box 2-3, the work of Catherine Lewis, in her book *Educating Hearts and Minds,* and the work of Robin Alexander, using videotapes to explore classroom culture and pedagogy in five cultures, are examples of this type of study. Although relatively large in scale, the Alexander study qualifies as Type III since it was not driven by the desire

BOX 2-3 Understanding Education Broadly:
Two Type III Studies

Educating Hearts and Minds. The research of Catherine Lewis (1995a, 1995b) provides insights into the Japanese approach to elementary education, which is designed to meet the needs of the whole child, for belonging, contribution, and intellectual competence. She argues that Japanese schools are successful in promoting students' academic achievement because by meeting these basic human needs, schools help children develop a positive attachment to schooling. Lewis bases her analysis on observations and interviews spanning 10 years in more than 30 elementary schools in three Japanese cities. She observed and interviewed teachers to explore why they used particular instructional techniques. Lewis outlines nine qualities of Japanese elementary education central to understanding Japanese achievement:

• whole-child education, including nonacademic subjects such as art and music;
• values-rich education, focusing on friendship, cooperation, and other aspects of social and emotional development;
• a caring, supportive community, with opportunities for students to get to know each other and to collectively shape classroom values and practices;
• learning to live in groups, through the use of *han,* or longer-term family-like groups with diverse abilities mixed together;
• reflection, or *hansei,* on goals either privately or collectively (in small groups or as a class), formally or informally;
• methods of discipline that promote a personal commitment to values;
• children's thinking helping to drive instruction and classroom life;
• "wet learning," a term used by the Japanese to describe approaches that are personal, emotional, and interpersonal (as opposed to "dry learning," which is logical, rational, and unemotional); and
• a standardized curriculum supportive of child inquiry.

SOURCES: Lewis (1995a, 1995b).

Culture and Pedagogy in Five Countries. Robin Alexander (2001) explores the effects of primary education on children's sense of empowerment using classroom videotapes from five countries: England, France, India, Russia, and the United States. Alexander's study compares four aspects of primary education in each culture: the structure and purposes, the thinking of teachers and the classroom experiences encountered by students, the relationship between the classroom and the world of educational and social policy, and the impact of culture and history. The multimethod analysis draws on data gathered in 1994-1998 at the system, school, and classroom levels, using interviews, observation, and videotape and audiotape, supplemented by school and country documentation, photographs, and daily journal entries.

The notion of cultures, as "the web of inherited ideas and values, habits and customs, institutions and world views which make one country, or one region, or one group, distinct from another," is paramount throughout the study (Alexander, 2001:5). Alexander acknowledges that although there may be cross-cultural similarities, educational policy and practice cannot be fully understood without reference to these distinctions. For example, he describes the nature of interactions between the levels studied, where classrooms, schools, and systems are microcultures in their own right, with inherent values and customs that also respond to external influences, and that offer a window onto the larger culture. The international nature of the study also enables him to study the processes by which ideas and practices migrate from one culture to another, such as when one country imposes practices on another through colonialism or when one country borrows practices from another.

SOURCE: Adapted from Alexander (2001).

either to compare achievement or to inform a specific policy. Such studies may be conducted by U.S. scholars in foreign countries or by foreign scholars in the United States and provide new ways of looking at familiar practices.

Private foundations pay for many of these studies, the cost of which is generally measured in tens or hundreds of thousands of dollars. In terms of indirect costs, Type III studies are undertaken only as expertise is available; they are often arranged between individual scholars or research groups and require minimal diplomatic capital. Because they deal with many fewer schools and smaller samples, they have relatively little impact on the time of students, teachers, and administrators. Type III studies that involve in-depth analysis of a single aspect of an education system can be relatively inexpensive in terms of both direct and indirect costs; unlike more expensive Type I and II studies, they often do not produce either generalizable findings or research methodologies capable of being precisely replicated in other jurisdictions. Instead, many offer rich descriptions of context in particular settings; these rich descriptions can provide clues to the variables influencing the phenomenon.

As a result, although they vastly outnumber Type I and Type II studies, Type III studies often do not come to the attention of policy makers or the public. This is a loss, since many are rich in narrative detail and paint a more engaging and provocative portrait of education in other countries than do the summary bar charts and graphs typical of many larger studies. Ethnographic and case studies, in particular, can explore cultural context in depth and, in turn, help elucidate the way education is organized and understood in different cultures. The detail these studies offer, however, renders them difficult to summarize, and their complexity often leads researchers to focus on just one or two countries, making their findings difficult to compare cross-nationally. The U.S. government currently has no formal priorities or budget for this type of study.

MOVING TOWARD A MORE BALANCED RESEARCH AGENDA

Establishing funding priorities for such a wide range of studies poses a challenge to all funders of international comparative education research. A balanced research agenda involves some support for basic statistics and indicators, other investments to address short- to medium-term policy concerns, and also significant investment in studies that explore broader issues in education over a longer period of time. Here the board suggests several criteria for developing a balanced, coherent research agenda. These criteria include investing in international studies that can help to address high-priority issues on the domestic research agenda; areas neglected to date by Type I studies; areas in which international research has a comparative advantage over domestic research; studies that respond to questions from a variety of positions and levels in the education system; and studies of the relative effectiveness of different methodologies in answering different types of questions and in communicating with different constituencies in the U.S. education system.

A part of the international comparative agenda should address some of the high-priority issues for domestic education research. Federally funded studies to date do this, to a limited extent, by focusing on Type I studies of achievement, in core curriculum areas, in formal K-12 schools, in countries perceived to be economic competitors of the United States. To the extent that these issues remain priorities for domestic education research and these international studies indeed are structured and timed in such a way that they are able to inform domestic research and policy, this current de facto international agenda is on target.

The domestic research agenda, however, is broader than the issues and methodologies evident in the de facto international research agenda. The list of high-priority domestic issues that could be illuminated by thoughtful research with international dimensions includes alternative assessment methods, finance, governance, teacher education, education at either end of the K-12 continuum, aspects of school outcomes other than achievement, closing the achievement gap between students from differing family backgrounds, and the school-to-work transition.

To take one example: the National Educational Research Policy and Priorities Board in the U.S. Department of Education identified as a priority finding ways to better serve the growing number of English language learners in U.S. schools (U.S. Department of Education, National Educational Research Policy and Priorities Board, 2000). This particular domestic research priority should be informed by international studies comparing other countries' experiences with second-language students and understanding of education systems in such geographic regions as Africa, Central and South America, and South Asia, which constitute the points of origin for large immigrant communities and many English language learners in U.S. schools. The weak state of education statistics in many of the countries in these regions means that many cannot participate in Type I studies in a meaningful way; fortunately, there is much to be learned about the children and parents who emigrate from these countries by means of other research methodologies.

Informing the domestic research agenda, however, should not be the only concern driving the international and comparative education research agenda. We should also reflect on how international comparative work can make unique contributions to basic understanding of the relationship between education and society. Because international research is so well positioned to reveal variation across societies, international comparative studies in education offer rich promise in deepening understanding of school-society relations and links between culture and schooling, religion and schooling, and the home and the school. In addition to those areas unevenly addressed by research (described above), these additional areas point to questions worth pursuing in future involvement in international studies.

Recommendation 1: Funding for international comparative education research should reflect a balance among the three types of international comparative education studies and should encompass a broad array of methodologies, scale, purposes, and topics. Specifically, the United States should increase investments in studies that focus on understanding the education experiences of other countries in their own context (Type II and Type III) to provide a broader context for U.S. experiences and efforts to innovate.

Yet another criterion for any research agenda for U.S. involvement in international comparative education studies is that it needs to include a range of questions generated from different originating points: addressing policy concerns, growing out of discipline-based theoretical concerns, accommodating and responsive to issues raised by other countries, and flowing from the experiences of practitioners. As elaborated in the following chapters, serious research is needed to uncover new ways of understanding education and good ideas for improving education should come from a variety of sources and flow in all directions among researchers, practitioners, parents, and students.

> **Recommendation 1.1: U.S. funders should foster closer links among practitioners and researchers so that both participate in the formulation and conduct of research, and both take responsibility for creating effective ways to use international education research.**

One way to ensure that international comparative education studies support and inform the domestic education research agenda is to encourage major domestic education research efforts to include an international component when that would add value to the domestic research findings. As do multimethod studies, international components work best when they are not simply contemporaneous add-ons to relatively complete domestic studies, but rather are executed in time to provide input at specific stages of the design, data collection, and analysis of domestic studies.

> **Recommendation 1.2: U.S. funders should routinely support international components in domestic (state, local, and national) education policy and practice studies that draw on experiences in other countries.**

MULTIPLE METHODOLOGIES

No single type of international comparative education study can answer all of the most pressing questions about how education works in other countries and how it might be improved in the United States. The most fruitful studies, however, are often those that combine multiple methodologies. For example, in the IEA Civic Education Study, case studies informed the design of frameworks for large surveys, which in turn generated correlations; these can now be explored by a range of other Type II and Type III studies tailored to specific geographic locations and contexts. At present, however, this sequencing of different types of related studies seems to be the exception rather than the rule. LeTendre (2002) argues that when multiple methods are used, an overarching framework for analysis that integrates results of the different research components strengthens the overall analytic power of any study. (We return to this topic in Chapter 5.)

Many scholarly debates about the validity, relevance, and generalizability of findings of international comparative education studies focus on the extent to which context has been recognized and properly taken into account in various aspects of the study. While randomized field trials and quasi-experimental designs are sometimes held up as the gold standard in domestic education research on effects of interventions, such methods can work only when in-depth knowledge of specific contexts allows researchers to model and control independent variables.

In many areas of international comparative studies, those who wish to pursue randomized field trials will need to invest in much exploratory, open-ended work in order to identify salient variables, comparable populations, and critical differences in environment. Can we understand the function of school exit exams or university entrance exams in different countries if we do not understand the income distribution and the returns to school attainment in those countries? Can we understand the early school performance of children without understanding the child-care and pre-school policies of a country? Patterns of income distribution and returns to school attainment must first be identified and the means to measure them must be developed before researchers can "control" them sufficiently to apply experimental methods. More support is needed for qualitative and historical studies, which, in addition to being valuable in and of themselves, can build the necessary foundation for further quantitative work.

Recommendation 1.3: U.S. funders should evaluate proposals for qualitative or historical studies and for quantitative studies by somewhat different criteria, conforming to fundamental principles of sound research for both and accommodating the different canons of systematic inquiry and different warrants for generalization in each discipline.

Although there is no single method of analysis that is agreed on by all international comparative education researchers, there is room for improvement in the methodologies of all three types of studies, and some component of any international comparative education research agenda should include studies to compare and improve research methodologies. Specific goals for improvement include organizing studies that use multiple methodologies in more effective ways. Designers and secondary data users could collaborate more effectively throughout the life of large-scale research studies to ensure greater use of the data. The use of videotaped studies of classrooms in other countries could be better understood. Findings from international comparative education studies could be used to stimulate better-informed discussions about education among U.S. policy makers and the public.

> **Recommendation 1.4: U.S. funders should encourage multicomponent research studies with longer time horizons, using a variety of qualitative and quantitative methodologies.**

In summary, because policy makers and educators in the United States cannot know in advance which studies will be critical, a prudent approach to developing a research agenda for international comparative studies in education is to support and encourage a broad range of study types and topics, with increased attention to those methodologies, topics, and geographical regions that have received relatively less investment in recent years, incorporating more international components into domestic studies, with some formative evaluations to study how domestic and international components can complement each other.

Finally, the scope of international comparative education studies means that no single set of methodological criteria will be adequate to evaluate the quality and promise of proposals for international comparative research and finished studies. As noted above, there is a continuing need for more qualitative and historical work that, while conforming to fundamental principles of sound research, is subject to different canons of systematic inquiry and different warrants for generalization than are large-scale surveys.

3

Impact

Determining the appropriate mix of different kinds of international comparative education studies requires not only an awareness of their scope and cost, but also a better understanding of the actual benefits and impact of different types of studies in the U.S. education community and the time frame necessary for that impact to be manifest. The United States, like many other countries, has participated in large-scale, cross-national education surveys assuming that comparative studies will, at some point, have a positive impact on its education system. Investments in smaller scale international comparative work by individuals and private groups are often similarly motivated.

Major investments in international comparative studies in education, however, are proceeding without analysis of these assumptions with respect to individual studies or programs of study. As in other areas of education research, gauging the actual impact of these studies—in terms of findings used, changes in student achievement, policies debated, understanding expanded—is difficult. Nonetheless, this chapter illustrates the many ways international comparative studies of all three types have had impact on the U.S education system and, with systematic effort, could have more. Our aim is not to use cost-benefit analysis to determine which studies should be funded and which dropped; rather, it is to understand when studies do in fact have impact and to reinforce them in those areas. Of course, the impact studies would also be valuable points of reference when new investment decisions are to be made as well.

Recommendation 2: The United States should conduct systematic analyses of costs of the expensive Type I and Type II studies (including financial cost, respondent or participant burden, accommodating dosing shortcomings, etc.) and benefits (services received, information provided, topics studies, etc.) so that a more complete picture of impact can inform future program and funding decisions. These analyses should be "internationally comparative" in that they compare impact in the United States with impact from the same or similar studies in other countries.

DEFINING IMPACT

The goals of the U.S. education system range from teaching such fundamental skills as reading, writing, and arithmetic to helping students begin a rewarding career and develop physically and emotionally (Cremin, 1990:42). With such a broad target, it might seem hard for education research to miss the mark. Nonetheless, the impact of education research—both domestic and international—remains difficult to measure.

Weiss (1998:331) defines impact as "the net effects of a program (i.e., the gains in outcomes for program participants minus the gain for an equivalent group of non-participants). Impact may also refer to program effects for the larger community." Measuring the impact of domestic or international education research findings on the U.S. education system, then, involves looking for costs and benefits for participants in different parts of the system and thinking about the system as a whole.

Take TIMSS as an example. Wiseman and Baker (2002) report that many *classroom teachers* who have encountered TIMSS perceive the results as implicitly critical of U.S. teachers, even as a challenge to their professionalism. In contrast, for *state and national policy makers*, TIMSS has been a more constructive experience, as many have been able to use poor performance on TIMSS 1995 and TIMSS 1999 to lobby for more funds for education. Similarly, for much of *the public*, TIMSS 1995 is history, but *researchers* only recently began to publish the results of secondary analyses addressing one or more of the myriad questions the study has raised. Finally, the influence of TIMSS 1995 on individual schools and school districts varied; although some higher achieving U.S. schools launched major reform efforts in response to the performance of the United States in TIMSS, the same data did not mobilize lower achieving U.S. schools into action (Wiseman and Baker, 2002).

International education research in the United States, like domestic research, suffers from a lack of infrastructure that could make research matter. Where do the results of research flow into the education system? Is the system too *loosely coupled* (Weick, 1976) to be influenced even by the strongest research findings? Raizen (2002) recounts how the United Kingdom and Singapore analyzed their performance on the Second International Science Study (SISS) and used the results to reform their science curriculum. Although the data do not allow an attribution of causality, she notes that both countries improved their performance dramatically in TIMSS; in contrast, Hong Kong undertook neither analyses of the SISS results nor curriculum reform and did not improve its performance in science between SISS and TIMSS. Raizen observes that, although many complained about the shallowness of U.S. mathematics and science curricula after the TIMSS results were released in 1996, there is little evidence of subsequent efforts to reduce coverage and deepen conceptual learning. Plank (2002), looking at the impact of international models on the U.S. debate on school choice and privatization, identifies the fragmented state of education decision making in the United States as one of the chief impediments to the effective use of education research about other countries. Since decentralized education decision making is highly prized in the United States, the task of getting policy-relevant findings to the decentralized level will continue to challenge both domestic and international education researchers for the foreseeable future.

Because of this fragmented decision making, international and domestic education studies are more likely to have an impact at the school or classroom level if design and analysis teams include representatives from the state and local levels and if the results can be disaggregated by state and locality. For example, TIMSS was a curriculum-based test administered to a national sample of classrooms, producing a distribution of scores around a national mean. Curriculum policy in the United States tends to be made at the state or local level, and benchmarking studies were attached to both TIMSS 1995 and TIMSS 1999, the latter allowing more than two dozen states, districts, and consortia to administer TIMSS as though their jurisdictions were countries. This located TIMSS results closer to the level at which the effects of curriculum decisions could be compared.

Type I studies tend to be the most expensive in terms of direct costs, as noted earlier, involving many individuals in the conduct of surveys and employing experts to organize and analyze them. But less often taken into account is that this type of study has high indirect costs as well and these should be taken into consideration when studies are planned and when impact is evaluated. These may include

- the burden on schools that sacrifice classroom and administrator time in order to participate in international assessments but typically gain little or nothing from them;
- the maintenance of the sophisticated infrastructure—data process-

ing centers, analysis units, training programs—needed to implement technically sound studies;

• the diplomatic capital needed to persuade a significant number of comparable countries to participate in a given assessment, with the desired level of sampling and measurement rigor;

• the opportunity cost, since adding studies reduces the amount of time that a limited number of experts in international large-scale assessment can spend on any single study; and

• undermining policy reform when studies are undertaken more frequently than policy reforms can produce change, creating the sense that policy reforms are not working.

Recommendation 2.1: U.S. funders should move away from piecemeal, ad hoc funding of international studies, and toward incorporating explicit considerations of relative cost, benefit, and impact in both the planning and the proposal review processes.

The flow of findings from domestic and international education studies into the U.S. education system is affected by factors that create a social and political environment more or less open to change. For example, after the mid-1980s many factors aided the rapid acceptance of the Reggio Emilia model by some in the U.S. early childhood education community (see Box 3-1). In the 1990s, an engaging traveling exhibition on the Reggio Emilia model exposed the public and teachers to a new way of organizing early childhood education in Italy. Many Americans who earlier had heard of another Italian preschool model, the Montessori method, were open to the possibility that the United States might have more to learn from Italy about early childhood education. The end of the cold war in the early 1990s also brought a greater level of comfort with ideas derived from groups who earlier might have been dismissed as European leftists. Interested scholars and educators from the United States would have found it easier to travel to Italy to observe Reggio Emilia than to travel to Japan or China.

Implementing the model in the United States did not involve changing legislation or even getting permission from a school board, since most early childhood education programs in the United States are privately rather than publicly organized. Early childhood educators interested in improving their instruction methods were in a position to try various models at will, knowing that their students would not face either mandatory exit exams from kindergarten or entry exams for elementary school. University-based scholars in the United States had studied the Reggio Emilia model in Italy and other countries and offered their expertise to some Reggio Emilia experiments in the United States.

BOX 3-1   The Reggio Emilia Approach to
Early Childhood Education

In the early 1960s, the parents in Reggio Emilia, a small, wealthy city in northern Italy, began developing an early childhood education program designed to take children seriously and to focus on nurturing collaboration and critical thinking as a means to prepare children for life in a democratic society. Inspired by a strong sense of purpose and civic engagement, Loris Malaguzzi, an Italian early education specialist, joined in the effort to open the first municipal preschool in 1963.

The Reggio Emilia philosophy of early childhood education is based on these key features:

• **The role of the environment as teacher:** The classroom, school, and its surroundings encourage discovery, involvement, and an interest in beauty and the environment.

• **Visual arts as means of representation:** Because of a belief that creativity is not a separate faculty but rather a way of thinking and responding to the world, collaborative partnerships are formed between classroom teachers and art educators to promote children's multiple means for expression.

• **Documentation as assessment and advocacy:** Documentation of student progress promotes adult (teacher and parent) understanding of and interest in children's development.

• **Long-term project work** or *progettazione*: Teachers guide children in gaining new insights through long-term projects that emerge from the child's interests.

• **Teacher as researcher:** Reggio Emilia educators use a Deweyian approach to scientific inquiry to guide classroom practice, i.e., posing hypotheses about children's learning, creating experimental conditions to test those hypotheses, collecting data (e.g., artifacts of children's work and transcripts of adult-child conversations), analyzing those data, and posing new hypotheses.

• **Education as relationship (adults and children, home and school):** The child, parents, and teachers all actively participate in the education process. Efforts are made to promote parent participation through building respectful home-school relationships. In the 1980s, Reggio Emila's influence began extending in other countries, particularly in the United States.

Since 1986, delegations of American early childhood educators have traveled to Reggio Emilia to observe the approach firsthand and to share those experiences with others at U.S. regional, state, and national conferences. Conference presentations and delegations helped to generate greater inter-

(continues)

BOX 3-1   Continued

est in Reggio Emilia and led to the establishment of formal and informal networks of teachers and teacher educators who began establishing their own study groups. The American media also helped get the word out through special features on public television and *Newsweek*'s declaration that Reggio Emilia preschool was "the best in the world" (Hinckle, 1991). Its widespread appeal stems in part from the guidance the approach gives teachers on how contemporary theories of how children learn can be translated into classroom practice. Reggio Emilia also affirms personal and professional values that take seriously both young children and early childhood educators.

SOURCE: Adapted from New (2002).

In addition, the model encouraged teachers and parents to undertake their own "action research," thereby legitimizing their role in and perhaps their commitment to developing their own programs. Further reinforcing the professional legitimacy of the program, Reggio Emilia now has its own set of sessions at the annual meetings of the National Association of Educators of Young Children and is considered a major curriculum model and educational approach in the literature of professional early childhood education (New, 2002). In this case, systematic scholarly studies did not play a role in spread of this innovation. Rather, Reggio Emilia-related activities offer an opportunity for comparative education researchers to respond to a practitioner-generated agenda by assessing the Reggio Emilia experience in the United States and how it can usefully, and perhaps necessarily, diverge from the program in Italy.

While the Reggio Emilia model has been influential among specialists in early childhood education, the extensive research on school choice and privatization in several other industrialized countries, widely reported in the academic and popular presses and synthesized in studies commissioned by the U.S. government, has not played a major role in the debate on choice and privatization in the United States (see Box 2-2). Plank (2002) relates this impotence in part to the equivocal findings of this research, and in part to the level of the education community at which this evidence might be used. Unlike the Reggio Emilia model, which could be adopted in whole or in part by educators at a classroom or a school level, the issue of choice opens up prospects of sweeping change in the allocation of control and resources at the district and state levels. Consequently, this animates powerful interest groups who may well be less interested in whether choice "works" in other countries than whether it challenges status quo interests. In the policy arena, international education research suffers the same fate as domestic research: strong evidence can be ignored in the formation of policy, and weak evidence can be deployed to support strong policy conclusions (Plank, 2002).

The popularity of Liping Ma's book *Knowing and Teaching Elementary Mathematics* (see Box 3-2) also provides another contrast that may shed some light on the lack of U.S. interest in international choice and privatization research. Fang (2002) argues that because Ma was writing as an outsider to U.S. education about a non-U.S. practice, her warm reception by partisans on both sides of the U.S. "math wars"[1] may be related in part to her perceived status as a neutral party. Ma, nonetheless, was able to explicitly compare Chinese with U.S. teachers, and the reception for her book by U.S. readers indicates it was hard to dismiss her work as another international study about an irrelevant country.

Despite the many similarities, international comparative education research does differ from domestic education research in several ways. First, comparative research demands attention to national as well as local contexts. The range of differences in schooling in various countries can hardly be imagined by many educators who have not spent significant time outside the United States. For secondary users to make sense of data about student achievement in other countries, comparative researchers must provide much background information and rich descriptions of context, elevating the importance of parallel case studies and of background variables. For these reasons, international research is likely to be more expensive than comparable domestic research. Finally, international educational research findings lend themselves more readily than domestic findings to rhetoric that plays to Americans' deep-rooted concerns about the relative competitiveness of the U.S. labor force, the economy, and the future of their children. The rhetoric surrounding international studies sometimes can lead to overestimates of the strength of reported findings and of their potential impact on classroom practice.

The following discussion of impact is loosely organized around five paths through which education research may influence the education system. Four of the paths lead to classroom practice: educational materials; pre- and in-service training for educators; education policies; and changed knowledge, attitudes, or practices among the public (National Research Council, 2002b). The fifth path leads to the domestic research community.

---

[1]The term "math wars" refers to controversies beginning in the early 1990s among various groups of mathematics educators and mathematicians regarding the proper emphasis on teaching (1) basic computational skills and (2) problem solving and advanced topics in mathematics.

BOX 3-2 Knowing and Teaching Elementary Mathematics

Knowing and Teaching Elementary Mathematics: Teachers' Understanding of Fundamental Mathematics in China and the United States by Liping Ma (1999) is based on a comparative study of knowledge of mathematics by Chinese and U.S. mathematics teachers. Ma interviewed teachers in both countries, and she paints a picture of their subject-matter knowledge about standard topics of elementary mathematics.

Ma depicts the differences in mathematics understanding between the two groups, with Chinese teachers tending to have a much more profound understanding of fundamental mathematics, that is, knowledge that enables teachers to go beyond computational accuracy and awareness of concepts to teach mathematical concepts to students. Ma describes factors that support the development of Chinese teachers' mathematical knowledge that do not exist in the United States, despite the fact that Chinese mathematics teachers typically receive less education than their U.S. counterparts. She concludes the book with suggestions for changes in teacher preparation and mathematics education to enable U.S. teachers to deepen their mathematics knowledge, such as enhancing the interaction between the study of mathematics as a subject and ways of learning how to teach it.

With 31,000 copies sold by the beginning of 2002, its publisher describes *Knowing and Teaching Elementary Mathematics* as a "runaway bestseller." Much of the book's popularity flows from its focus on issues of current concern in the U.S. education community and also from the clarity of its argument. About the time of the book's release, the National Council of Teachers of Mathematics was in the process of updating its 1989 mathematics curriculum, assessment, and professional development standards. Both sides in the so-called math wars,* no longer able to discuss dispassionately what constitutes basic skills and conceptual understanding in mathematics or how best to teach them, found evidence and arguments in the book to support their positions. Even though the findings were not entirely new, Liping Ma presented them in a way that resonated with both sides.

Ma's life story contributed significantly to the development of her research and ultimately her book. Ma grew up in urban Shanghai, but during the Cultural Revolution, after receiving only eight years of formal school-

*Between 1992 and 2002, with funding from the National Science Foundation (NSF) and NCES, the board published four reports on the results, use, secondary analysis, and effects of TIMSS, all of them with many caveats and recommendations about the implications of TIMSS for policy and practice. In addition, the board sponsored a public symposium and published an edited volume, based on the symposium, on methodological advances in the methodology of cross-national achievement studies (including TIMSS) and a report on the methodology and use of videotapes in cross-national studies, prompted by the TIMSS Videotape Classroom Study.

ing, was sent to teach in a rural village. In Jiangxi, she taught for seven years and then served as the school's principal and later as the county's education superintendent. After the Cultural Revolution, Ma studied at the East China Normal University, a national university that plays a leading role in teacher preparation, where she read world classics in education, such as Confucius, Rousseau, and Zahkob. Her passion for education led her to study education research and teaching at Michigan State University. She began work on a teacher research project in the National Research Center for Teacher Education to help pay for her education. While coding interviews with U.S. elementary teachers about mathematics, she noticed some differences between U.S. and Chinese teachers' understanding of mathematics. The center provided a $1,000 grant for Ma to return to China and collect data. These data later became the foundation for her dissertation at Stanford University and for the 1999 book.

The impact of the book has been widespread yet disparate, affecting the research community more than practitioners. The mathematics community played an important role in disseminating the book, which has been adopted at the university level for mathematics courses but has had limited impact in teacher preparation programs. The Conference Board of the Mathematical Sciences drew on Ma's ideas about teachers' deep, profound, and connected mathematical knowledge to describe the content and pedagogical knowledge it recommended that U.S. mathematics teachers acquire during preservice training. The book's ideas have affected some school districts and teachers. The California Subject Matter Project includes a professional development component for mathematics that helps teachers develop the profound understanding Ma describes. The Mid-Atlantic Eisenhower Consortium for Mathematics and Science Education at Research for Better Schools has also promoted Ma's ideas through its professional development workshops. The far-reaching influence of Ma's work illustrates how small-scale comparative studies can have a powerful impact on educational research and practice.

SOURCES: Fang (2002); Ma (2002).

EVIDENCE OF IMPACT

The examples scattered throughout this chapter illustrate many ways in which comparative studies can change classroom practice and ideas about education. Examining intellectual histories and antecedents of these cases, the board found a surprising degree of connection among these studies. These connections suggest that the impact of international studies is sometimes recursive. For example, TIMSS 1995 played a role in opening U.S. educators' eyes to instructional methods used in other countries, particularly in mathematics and science, and particularly in high-performing countries, such as Singapore (see Box 2-2). *The Learning Gap* (Stevenson and Stigler, 1992), which compares mathematics education in China, Japan, and the United States, as well as the relatively high performance of Asian countries on TIMSS 1995, prepared some in the U.S. mathematics community to absorb Liping Ma's insights about the superior knowledge base of elementary mathematics teachers in China and to seize the Singapore mathematics curriculum. The TIMSS videotapes, which were widely used in professional development, and *The Teaching Gap* (Stigler and Hiebert, 1999), a book based on the TIMSS Videotape Classroom Study, motivated educators to take a closer look at Japanese lesson study. The impact of studies and innovations on U.S. education policy and practice, however, has been mixed, as described below.

Educational Materials

Curriculum documents, lesson plans, textbooks, and computer programs are among the most easily transported, interpreted, and analyzed means of changing what goes on in classrooms. Their appropriate interpretation, however, requires a deeper understanding of the education system in which those materials play only a supporting role. Different curricula assume different levels of expertise on the part of the teachers, different frequency and length of classes, different preparation and extracurricular support for learning, and a host of other factors.

The first and second IEA mathematics and science studies were among the first large-scale achievement surveys to attempt to seek a connection between the curriculum topics teachers said they taught and student performance on achievement surveys. The First International Mathematics Study (FIMS) introduced the concept of "opportunity to learn"; the Second International Mathematics Study (SIMS) contributed the concept of "enacted curriculum"; and it was in connection with TIMSS curriculum analysis that Americans learned to think about their K-12 curricula as "a mile wide and an inch deep" (Dossey, 2002). These changes have stimulated U.S. educators to reexamine their own and other countries' curricula, although not necessarily to the extent of the United Kingdom and Singapore, mentioned above, and not necessarily combined with efforts to derive hypotheses from the TIMSS data about what sorts of curricula might be more effective. The United States was not alone in its lack of attention to and support for this task; Postlethwaite (1999:60) writes, "It was the crude achievement results that had an impact in terms of awakening the [U.K. education] ministry personnel to the shortcomings of a region or country."

Wiseman and Baker (2002:i) assert that American response to TIMSS has been more reactive than interpretive. When TIMSS 1995 placed U.S. students near the mean in international mathematics and science assessments, some U.S. educators made a direct connection between curriculum and performance and promptly acquired copies of the curriculum used in the highest performing country, Singapore (see Box 2-2). Singapore's textbooks, written for English-language schools, were accessible to English-speaking Americans and appeared to offer a more sequential, structured approach to teaching mathematics than most U.S. textbooks at the time. Meanwhile, a few years after TIMSS was released, Singapore itself changed its textbooks, reducing the content and increasing the emphasis on problem-solving and critical thinking (Lee and Fan, 2002).

Several cases highlight the important role played by artifacts—actual textbooks from Singapore, children's artwork in the Reggio Emilia traveling exhibit—in documenting techniques, as opposed to abstract concepts. Understanding the power of such artifacts, the Council for Basic Education's Schools Around the World[2] program recently began giving a small group of teachers in nine countries the opportunity to compare examples of student work on similar subjects and problems. The TIMSS Toolkit[3] includes the official English translation of the Japanese Ministry of Education's National Course of Study for Mathematics (Peak et al., 2002) and a videotape of actual mathematics lessons in Germany, Japan, and the United States. Finally, in an approach somewhere between adapting another country's curriculum and trying to learn from another's artifacts, in 2000, Houghton Mifflin, a U.S. textbook publisher, hired Liping Ma and her collaborator to develop a U.S. mathematics curriculum supplement informed by their research on the different ways U.S. and Chinese teachers communicate profound understanding of fundamental mathematics (Fang, 2002).

Teacher Development

There are many ways in which teacher development can be influenced by international research and in which teachers can, in turn, inform international research. As described in Box 3-3, *The Teaching Gap* (Stigler and Hiebert, 1999) combined with the TIMSS Videotape Classroom Study to

---

[2]Council for Basic Education, Washington, D.C. (http://www.c-b-e.org).

[3]Attaining Excellence: A TIMSS Resource Kit, commonly known as the "TIMSS Toolkit," was prepared by the U.S. Department of Education to share some of the highlights of TIMSS with U.S. practitioners. It includes modules on TIMSS as a starting point to examine mathematics assessments, U.S. education, student achievement, teaching, and curricula (U.S. Department of Education, Office of Educational Research and Improvement, 1997).

BOX 3-3   Impact of Japanese Lesson Study in the United States

Lesson study, or *jugyokenkyu*, is a process of professional development that evolved during the period of progressive education reform in Japan following World War II, a time when the focus was on teacher-directed work on curriculum development and child-centered education (Yoshida, 1999). The process begins when a group of teachers, either from the same school or from different ones, comes together to work toward a common goal they want to achieve, usually to address a gap they have identified in students' current knowledge or ability. Working on lesson study involves several steps that incorporate both observation and collaboration, and yield a written record of the insights gained from watching lessons unfold in a real classroom.

The goal of the lesson study process is to help teachers become more deliberate and self-aware in their teaching practice and to carry insights gained from group planning into their daily individual lesson planning and teaching practice. The process is designed to be teacher-driven; teachers select the topic to be studied, identify the goal of the lesson, and learn from each other's experiences and expertise.

The history of lesson study in the United States began in the 1980s and 1990s, when the process came to the attention of several U.S. education scholars through their ongoing research into Japanese approaches to teaching. Catherine Lewis became aware of lesson study through her observations in Japanese elementary classrooms (see Box 2-3). James Stigler became aware of lesson study during his research on an NSF-funded study using videotapes of Japanese and U.S. teaching. In 1993-1994, Stigler and his graduate student Clea Fernandez directed a lesson study group in the United States with a group of teachers from the University of California Los Angeles Lab School. Makoto Yoshida, a doctoral student of Stigler's collecting data on lesson study in Japan, served as their main source of information for guiding U.S. teachers through the process.

The TIMSS Videotape Classroom Study, with its images from Japanese classrooms, piqued broad interest in Japanese approaches to teaching mathematics. Stigler and James Hiebert published the findings from TIMSS for a broad audience in *The Teaching Gap* (1999) and, through this work, lesson study emerged both as an important tool for understanding the culture of teaching in Japan and a potentially beneficial strategy in the U.S. education context.

To deepen understanding about lesson study and to explore its impact in U.S. schools, in 1999 Fernandez, now a professor at Teachers' College at Columbia University, and Yoshida began working with Paterson Public School #2 in New Jersey in collaboration with the Mid-Atlantic Eisenhower Consortium and the Japanese School of Greenwich, Connecticut. The first large-scale open house took place in 2000 with 150 attendees from the

Association of Mathematics Teachers from across the United States. Over time, a number of lesson-study groups were formed. In 2000, Delaware implemented one of the first statewide initiatives for lesson study; at the same time, Bellevue School District in Washington instituted one of the first district-wide initiatives. At the time of this writing, 25 states are represented in the roster of lesson-study clusters, covering at least 60 school districts and over 200 schools.

Those involved have suggested reasons why lesson study might work well in the United States. It is a commonsense idea that fits into U.S. thinking about educational reform. Lesson study professionalizes teaching through its focus on improving teaching practice, with teachers controlling their own professional development through concrete, classroom-based activity. At the same time, obstacles to its adoption in the United States include such logistical concerns as time, bureaucratic details, and money; the need for more in-depth understanding of the process; cultural limitations, such as the idea that peer observation is threatening to many U.S. teachers; and systemic issues, such as the pressure for accountability demonstrable through achievement scores.

A tension exists in the United States between the appeal of and resistance to things Japanese. Because of Japan's higher results on TIMSS and on other international assessments, there is an impulse to emulate successful strategies. Those trying to introduce lesson study here, however, face some resistance from U.S. educators who believe that the cultural differences are too great to allow lesson study to work in the United States. The question remains whether lesson study can be as successful a grassroots movement in the United States as it has been in Japan.

SOURCE: Chokshi (2002). For more information, see, for example, Fernandez (2002) and Lewis and Tsuchida (1998).

prompt a wave of practitioner-level interest in Japanese lesson study. Chokshi (2002) argues that lesson study caught on among practitioners because it is a commonsense idea, appealing to teachers' sense of professionalism, teacher-controlled, able to fill gaps in teachers' skills, and a concrete rather than a theoretical activity. Chokshi also reports, however, that several researchers working with teachers to operationalize and adapt lesson study anticipate that several factors will make it difficult to adapt to the U.S. context beyond the pilot phase:

- teachers' general lack of time for professional development not already programmed by the school or district;
- lack of the necessary expertise in the practitioner community with

respect to implementing this approach, leading to a need for experts to assist teachers in organizing and conducting lesson-study activities;

• cultural limitations, such as U.S. teachers' reluctance, relative to Japanese teachers, to allow others to observe or evaluate their teaching;

• current policy emphasis on standards and accountability not amenable to teachers' experiments to increase opportunity to learn or on gradual efforts to change classroom practice; and

• lack of long-term perspective among school administrators and teachers, related to the U.S. focus on quick results.

Although pre- and in-service professional development programs are important conduits for communicating findings from international comparative education research to teachers, practitioners may on their own initiative seek and try out international innovations that only later attract the attention of scholars and policy makers. At times, scholarly international comparative studies or professional development materials may be the second or third step in the process of introducing an international innovation to the United States, and the early-adapting teachers in the United States may provide some of the primary data for those studies. For example, as with any innovation, teachers or school boards who may have a limited understanding of the context of an international model will make sense of the model in their own terms, adapting it in ways that strengthen or weaken the effects intended by the model's developers.

As communication technologies continue to improve, and more educational materials are posted on the Internet, one can expect to see more direct grassroots borrowing of educational methods from one country to another. The TIMSS 1995 videotapes of mathematics lessons in three countries were powerful demonstrations to U.S. mathematics teachers of how different their teaching approaches could be and motivated many to adapt their instruction (Bunt, 2001). As a result, science educators insisted that science classrooms be included along with mathematics classrooms in the TIMSS-R Videotape Study.

Both the Organisation for Economic Co-operation and Development (OECD) and the International Association for the Evaluation of Educational Achievement (IEA) are in the process of launching new, large, cross-nationally comparative studies of teacher education. These studies also are likely to increase teachers' exposure to and opportunities to experiment with teaching practices from other countries.

Policy

The demand for TIMSS 1995 originated with policy makers who wanted to know how U.S. students compared academically with their peers in other countries. In reviewing just a few of many U.S. activities undertaken following the release of the TIMSS data in 1996, Wiseman and Baker (2002) note several impacts in the United States, which include

- increasing the impetus for reform, rather than increasing reform capacity, per se;
- stirring policy makers into action at the national and state levels but discouraging educators at lower levels in the education system;
- providing a benchmark for the education system;
- increasing the quantity of domestic education research; and
- contributing to an improved understanding of the basic nature of the education system.

At the same time, Wiseman and Baker also conclude that response to TIMSS has tended to be

- direct rather than interpretive,
- reactive rather than reflective,
- concentrated in high-performing jurisdictions, and
- having more impact on professional development than on scholarly or policy analysis.

These conclusions are consistent with the work of Weiss (1991), who argues that research presented as *data* is usually too dense and indirect to inform policy makers who are not already in agreement on values and goals, particularly when alternative policies are not sharply drawn and the situation is changing slowly. Indeed, TIMSS was more often simplified into *ideas* and *arguments* that Weiss points out are particularly influential when existing policy is in disarray, uncertainty is high, and policy makers are looking for legitimization after decisions have been made in a decentralized policy arena.

Participants in a Board on Comparative Studies in Education (BICSE) symposium reflecting on the results of TIMSS (National Research Council, 1999) expressed concern that the results would be translated into quick fixes. They emphasized that the picture of the U.S. education system provided by TIMSS was an incomplete snapshot of the state of U.S. schools at one point in time. The test covered only that part of the U.S. curriculum that was common with the curriculum of other participating countries and did not represent necessarily a balanced picture of the entire U.S. curriculum. U.S. educators who have taken the TIMSS curriculum framework or the test as a basis for their own work have not always been aware of the lack of balance and completeness.

Nevertheless, policy makers interviewed in connection with several of the background papers recently prepared for the board said they were convinced that TIMSS has made a significant impact on standards and assessment (Raizen, 2002; Wiseman and Baker, 2002). Rothman (2002) traces the movement toward constructing educational assessments tied to content standards, which began in the United States in the early 1990s when President George H.W. Bush announced the National Education Goals and state governors pledged that the United States would be "first in the world" in mathematics and science by the year 2000. Throughout the 1990s, the National Education Goals Panel, composed of governors, business leaders, administration officials, and members of Congress, monitored the progress toward this national goal using comparisons with international studies. By 2001, the United States had clearly failed to meet the goals and the panel was disbanded. Work on benchmarking standards with international data continues on a state-by-state basis through the nonprofit organizations Achieve and McREL.[4] After TIMSS, school districts working with the Council of Great City Schools were more willing to participate in the National Assessment of Educational Progress (Sharon Lewis, personal communication, April 2002), and discussions of a voluntary national test took on new life (Lois Peak, personal communication, April 2002).

Much of the story in the preceding paragraph, however, could be construed as policy mischief brought about by government officials determined to increase funding for education and armed with an extremely powerful piece of rhetoric: cross-national comparisons of education performance based on national averages. National comparisons tend to be more valid when countries have national education systems and centralized decision making. In the United States, however, more than 14,000 school districts vary enormously in terms of curriculum, funding, and performance.

For example, *A Nation at Risk* used the mean performance level of U.S. students on SIMS, an international study with notoriously weak sampling standards, to convince Americans that there was a generalized crisis of poor quality in the U.S. school system. This crisis was used to promote standards and led directly to the formation of the National Education Goals Panel. Berliner and Biddle (1995) call this a "manufactured crisis," on the grounds that the performance of many U.S. students is comparable to those in high-performing countries. They argue the U.S. crisis lies in the low performance of a subset of schools and students, and therefore

---

[4]Achieve and McREL (Mid-continent Research for Education and Learning) have collaborated to "help states implement high academic standards by providing access to comprehensive standards-based resources," http://frodo.mindseye.com/achieve/achievestart.nsf/OutsideSearch.

response to this crisis should be focused on those schools and students, rather than generalized to the entire U.S. education system.[5] Nonetheless, U.S. officials used the mean performance level of U.S. students on TIMSS 1995 to impress on Americans once again that U.S. schools in general were not "first in the world."

Mathematics and science educators are less convinced that TIMSS has had significant impact on their fields. Raizen (2002) explains that the U.S. national science standards were completed before TIMSS was released. Dossey (2002) observes that the middle school mathematics standards proposed by Achieve and McREL appear to be directly linked to TIMSS 1995 results, but those results simply reiterate the findings of the earlier FIMS and SIMS studies using more compelling data.

Policy makers are sometimes tempted to use international achievement trend studies to evaluate policy reforms (National Research Council, 2002a). However, synchronizing the attention span of the political world (1 year or less), the current cycle between international education assessments (3 or 4 years), the time needed to create a critical mass of peer-reviewed research findings (5 to 10 years), and the cycle of education reform (perhaps decades) remains a problem. Nonetheless, understanding the interaction of these four different cycles, and the funding cycles that constrain them, is a central imperative for all education research in the United States, domestic or international. Four years after TIMSS 1995, U.S. students did not manifest a significant gain on TIMSS 1999, and the results were released with little fanfare. Was it too early to detect any effects of reform? Was there not a critical mass of U.S. education jurisdictions engaged in a common reform effort, on a common schedule? Did different jurisdictions with different performances effectively cancel out each other's effects? Even had the United States made significant gains, one journalist suggested, officials might be reluctant to showcase international education studies in which U.S. students perform well, such as reading and civic education, given that requests for budget increases are easier to defend when they are tied to crises, rather than to strong performances (Berliner and Biddle, 1995; Rothman, 2002).

Recommendation 2.2: U.S. funders should give highest priority, of all the possible impact studies that might be undertaken, to an impact analysis of TIMSS 1995. This analysis should address TIMSS in terms of (a) its efforts to serve as both an indicator and a research study and (b) its impact on the U.S. education system.

---

[5]A recent report on educational disadvantage in 24 industrialized countries, using data from the Programme for International Student Assessment 2000 and TIMSS 1999, consistently places the United States in the bottom third of all countries (United Nations Children's Fund, 2002).

The Public

Like teachers, the public both influences and is influenced by international research. Some examples illustrate the complex balance between research and public perceptions. In her review of three Japanese instructional practices currently used in the United States—the Suzuki method of music instruction, the Japanese system of martial arts instruction, and the *kumon* method of mathematics instruction—Peak (2002) identified five stages in the U.S. institutionalization of these innovations: initial interest, try out existing materials, exchange master teachers, adopt a few techniques, and create a full U.S. version. These five stages echo some of the innovations described in this report, including the Reggio Emilia traveling exhibit containing artifacts of young children's classroom work and the lesson-study scholars linking Japanese teachers with U.S. teachers.

Now that TIMSS shows students in less affluent and less developed Asian countries consistently outperforming their peers in the United States, the U.S. public may be more open to ideas and practices from other countries than it has been in the recent past. Such receptivity was harder to sustain as the U.S. economy prospered in the late 1990s, when the Asian countries that had performed particularly well on TIMSS were struggling through economic downturns. This caused some to question the often-asserted link between high performance on international mathematics and science assessments and high national performance in the global economy.

In trying to understand the impact of TIMSS 1995 on discourse in the U.S. education community, several individuals[6] who participated in the TIMSS 1995 release and public relations process attributed great importance to releasing the data with much fanfare and embedding them in a coherent "story line" already developed by one research group granted early access to the data. Such fanfare for a single story line, however, runs the risk of becoming a "policy trap," as noted by LeTendre et al. (2001:1):

> The early release of TIMSS reports, combined with pre-existing political agendas and educational reform movements, created conditions where univariate distributions were interpreted as "hard data," first in the media and later in policy debates, eventually undermining the ability of later, secondary analysis to impact reform initiatives.

Such policy traps are not unique to TIMSS (Wineburg, 1997a, 1997b) and were avoided by several other countries participating in TIMSS by

---

[6]Larry Suter, National Science Foundation, and William Schmidt, Michigan State University. Personal communications, 2001-2002.

planning secondary analysis at the time the study was designed. By comparison, in the United States, according to David Baker, "secondary is often perceived as second-class analysis" (personal communication, April 17, 2002). Studies that reveal a perceived problem in the U.S. education system tend to galvanize responses from teachers and parents associated with schools that have enough resources to craft and implement a response. By the time the early findings of a large study are challenged or overturned by peer-reviewed secondary analysis, public interest in the study has probably waned.

Raizen suggested another effect of TIMSS 1995 and TIMSS 1999 benchmarking studies on the public: with the elite First-in-the-World[7] consortium schools performing at the level of the highest performing countries and the Miami-Dade county schools performing at the level of such developing countries as Turkey (Mullis et al., 1998), the benchmarking studies helped to drive home to the public the bifurcation of the U.S. education system into high- and low-performing schools. In this case, such findings help call attention to an aspect of the U.S. school system that is taken for granted by many Americans, and that is a distinguishing factor in comparison with schools in other industrialized countries.

Education journalists report that TIMSS 1995 and other international study results in recent years have caused both journalists and the public to be more critical of the U.S. school system (Rothman, 2002). Although TIMSS 1995 is mentioned most frequently in this regard, journalists also mentioned a study of the voucher system in New Zealand (Fiske and Ladd, 2000) and an OECD study on graduation rates in developed countries, which challenged the prevailing notion that the United States educates a greater proportion of its population than any other nation.

Recommendation 2.3: U.S. funders should support reviews of the impact of different study methodologies on different audiences.

The Research Community

Historically, the U.S. education research community owes much to comparative education studies. Although a recent history of education research in the United States (Lagemann, 2000) contains very few references to foreign innovations and research, during the 19th and early 20th centuries, John Dewey and other leading American thinkers took ex-

---

[7]First in the World is a collaboration between 18 school districts in the United States that aim to become first in the world in mathematics and science. http://www.1stintheworld.org.

tended study tours of Europe and Russia to observe foreign education systems and practices, and many earned degrees from foreign universities. From 19th century England, U.S. educators borrowed the idea of factory-like classrooms to address urban mass education; from France and Germany, the idea of early childhood education; and from 20th century Japan, the Suzuki method of music instruction, to name just a few of the internationally derived innovations that contributed to the development of the U.S. education system.

These and many other popular innovations, however, were instructional and organizational techniques that practitioners could observe, apply, and adapt more or less successfully, without extensive input from formal researchers. Today more than half of the scholarly education researchers in the world are based in the United States, and in the last half of the 20th century Americans placed increasing emphasis on the scientific, quantitative study of education processes. But as education research becomes more technically sophisticated, it often becomes more complex, less accessible to practitioners, and less likely to affect instructional and organizational reform directly.

Comparative education research in the past 15 years has, however, had an impact on the direction and abundance of domestic education research in the United States. Wiseman and Baker (2002) cite the importance of *A Splintered Vision: An Investigation of U.S. Science and Mathematics Education* (Schmidt, McKnight, and Raizen, 1997) in delving into curriculum questions that educational researchers had been asking for decades, but only TIMSS had the data to explore. They also cite the peer-reviewed publications of the Secondary Analysis of TIMSS Project at Pennsylvania State University; of those published between 1997 and 2002, six out of nine appeared in journals with primarily domestic audiences.

The availability for secondary analysis of a dataset of the size and quality of TIMSS and the 2001 Civic Education Study has not been lost on younger scholars. Raizen estimates that 20 to 25 percent of American Educational Research Association fellowship proposals are based on research on TIMSS. Other observers attribute increased interest in curriculum studies in the 1990s, particularly the emphasis on mathematics and science, to issues arising from FIMS, SIMS, and TIMSS. The TIMSS videotapes certainly contributed to increased interest in studying teacher preparation and professionalism (Dossey, 2002). The other studies and innovations covered by the cases highlighted in the boxes through this chapter are much smaller, and their impact on research is difficult to track. Some high-profile, practitioner-driven efforts in the United States to try out internationally derived innovations, such as the Singapore mathematics curriculum and the Reggio Emilia early childhood program, may have the effect of getting some practitioner issues on the education research agenda.

Foreign graduate students, such as Liping Ma, and foreign-born schol-ars, such as John Ogbu of Nigeria, can play an important role in introduc-ing new questions and ideas for domestic researchers in U.S. schools of education. Lee Shulman explained that this "comes to the heart of why comparative work is so important." He views Ma's book as a dramatic instance of the proposition that international work allows the outsider to see something insiders take for granted and, in the process, make it inter-esting, problematic, and worthy of investigating for insiders (Fang, 2002:13).

IMPLICATIONS

This brief, illustrative review contains many ideas for increasing the use and usability of international comparative education studies. Differ-ent types of studies have had different effects, within different time frames, on different parts of the education system. Our examples illus-trate the need to look at impact at several levels of the education system. In order to reach specific groups or levels in the system most effectively, it may be necessary to incorporate them into the design both of studies and of analyses. The social and political environment affects openness to ideas from abroad; current concerns about globalization among many Ameri-cans may be elevating levels of interest in education systems in other coun-tries. Innovations and study findings from other countries that focus on techniques and practices may be more quickly absorbed and adapted than may policy changes. Scholars who can explicitly connect their research on education in other countries to education practices and phenomena in the United States may make more of an impact than those that make no such explicit comparisons with the United States. Foreign scholars may have some comparative advantage in helping Americans talk construc-tively about education issues that have become polarized in domestic de-bate. Artifacts and videotapes may have a particularly important role in helping Americans move beyond preconceived notions of the possible and impossible in education.

These examples also raise many questions: could international com-parative researchers be doing more to work with U.S. practitioners to evaluate practitioner-driven, internationally inspired innovations in U.S. schools? The Reggio Emilia experiments certainly call for this, and the collaboration between lesson-study practitioners and researchers demon-strates how this might be accomplished. In the United States, there is perpetual tension between asynchronous cycles of decentralized politics, research, and education reform; do other countries with decentralized education systems manage these tensions better? Can we match up young researchers attracted by the vast datasets produced by Type I studies to states and districts that do not have the time or expertise to analyze their benchmarking data?

> **Recommendation 2.4: U.S. funders should support reviews of the impact of ongoing and completed international comparative studies on the practice of education on a planned and continuing basis to determine how effects can be enhanced.**

In summary, those looking for ways to balance investments in different types of international comparative education research should consider more factors than cost and topics. These additional factors include the expected and actual benefits of similar, earlier studies; the time frame needed to realize those benefits; negative effects, such as creating an unduly negative picture of the U.S. education systems; and the relative effectiveness of different types of study designs and methodologies in producing "useable" research for different audiences in parts of the education system. These factors are not presently well understood in the education research community and in themselves constitute areas for increased education research funding.

4

New Directions

Despite the emphasis thus far on developing a research agenda more balanced among Types I, II, and III, this chapter contains more specific recommendations for Type I studies than for any other type. This is because the preponderance of the board's work over the past 10 years has been focused on Type I studies. This sustained focus on Type I studies has impressed on the board not only the importance of Type I studies, but also their limitations and potential abuses and the need for monitoring and evaluating these major investments. Moreover, this concentration has convinced the board of the need for systematic, increased investments in Type II and III studies that can both inform Type I studies and go beyond what they can achieve. Type II and III studies are essential for expanding our understanding about how education can and does work and in exploring questions about context between and within countries that Type I studies cannot yet begin to operationalize. As for ways to improve Type II and III studies, more specific recommendations should be based on more experience with funding such studies on a more systematic and broader scale.

GETTING MORE FROM TYPE I STUDIES

Large-scale, cross-national Type I surveys have dominated U.S. funding for international comparative education research for the past 15 years and, even in a more balanced portfolio, are likely to continue to represent a large proportion of the total budget. Several issues affect the degree of utility that Type I studies can offer; most important are the ways in which they are coordinated and monitored with each other and with other types of studies. The board considers that much has been learned from the conduct of past studies, and in this chapter we lay out our recommendations for improving the conduct of future Type I studies.

The emphasis on Type I studies in the 1990s was a logical response to the way that results of earlier surveys of dubious technical quality (U.S. Department of Education, National Center for Education Statistics, 1994) dominated U.S. education policy debates in the late 1980s. Education analysts at the National Center for Education Statistics and the National Science Foundation led the effort to secure the massive funding necessary to raise the quality of the 1990s round of educational achievement surveys in order to establish more rigorous, representative comparisons and raise the quality of discourse about the U.S. education system and its relationship to those in other countries.

The board's report *Methodological Advances in Cross-National Surveys of Educational Achievement* (National Research Council, 2002a) explores the consensus among leading experts regarding technical improvements in assessing student achievement over the past four decades. In the construction of achievement tests, the report concludes that psychometric advances in differential item functioning, translation procedures, and clearer standards for item statistics represent significant improvements. Best practices in international assessment have been codified to some extent in documents such as the *Technical Standards* of the International Association for the Evaluation of Educational Achievement (IEA) (Martin et al., 1999) and *Measuring Student Knowledge and Skills: A New Framework for Assessment* of the Organisation for Economic Co-operation and Development (OECD, 1999). Improvements in sampling and in documentation have generated increased confidence in survey findings. Computer technology has radically increased the amount of data that can be managed by one survey, as well as the level of effort needed to do it. Recent surveys also include better measures of social background (in the Second International Mathematics Study and the Programme for International Student Assessment (PISA), less so in TIMSS), valuable data on opportunity to learn, and more powerful inferences drawn from increasingly complex statistical analyses of achievement data.

Room for improvement is also evident in several areas in Type I studies. By discussing this topic, the board does not necessarily imply that some studies were designed or have been implemented badly. Rather, the experience of implementing past studies has brought to light many new issues and dilemmas that now need to be addressed. For example, areas for improvement for TIMSS include: using the study components to strategically inform each other; integrating the mathematics and science portions of the survey; incorporating advances in measurement of opportunity to learn, social background, and other independent variables into successive studies; appreciating the importance of *distributions* of achievement as well as achievement *levels*; and gaining flexibility in adapting to the needs and findings of secondary analysis. Many of these issues are related to the decision to make TIMSS into a trend study, to be repeated every four years. Others are related to larger issues of coordination, discussed below. Finally, to date, TIMSS has been unable to resolve the sampling and response rate problems that rendered TIMSS 1995 cohort III (12th grade) largely unusable.

One of the purposes of the *1990 Framework* was to help set technical standards for the few international studies in which the United States had an opportunity to participate. Today, with the improvements in technical standards and the proliferation of studies cited throughout this report, the pivotal issue in the U.S. decision to participate in any given study is the potential impact of the study in light of its costs and the extent to which it fits into a systematic plan. The need for such a plan is highlighted by the current confusing array of Type I studies under way or under development, with similar topics, overlapping implementation schedules, and little reference to each other. This confusion persists because the decision-making process with respect to funding individual studies has been relatively ad hoc. To date, Type I studies lack coordination from a body that is (a) relatively independent of the particular Type I studies themselves, (b) willing and able to identify and prioritize supporting Type II and III studies, (c) able to make choices and to foster channels of communication among various studies, and (d) able to find ways to channel the results of such research into the national educational discourse.

Recommendation 3: On a continuing basis, the federal government should plan, coordinate, monitor, and modify studies in the government's portfolio of international comparative education research.

Coordination

In many public policy domains, coordination and collaboration are the ideal, not the norm. Competition for resources is fierce; careers are made by investing in one approach and shunning others. While the technical quality of international large-scale research has improved dramatically during the previous decade, with the growth in the number of Type I studies comes an increase in the importance of political issues. Who determines which topics are studied? Who defines the research questions? Who supports which components? Whose agenda is being advanced? Who controls it? How much data will they share? When? To what degree is diplomatic capital needed and deployed? Who decides whether one large study is more appropriate than a dozen smaller ones? Methodological improvements do not address these questions. Moreover, if one research group or country does not deal respectfully with others' concerns early in the design process, then the best technical standards in the world will not guarantee broad agreement on the validity of the final results.

For example, to date most Type I studies have not been designed by groups broadly representative of the international comparative education research community and have not integrated practitioner, student, and parent concerns into their work. As a result, Type I study designs often do not reflect critical debates in the social science research community about how knowledge is defined and distributed and how that process reproduces inequality in society. As a result, Type I studies are often of little interest to the scholars most capable of designing the Type III studies that may well explain Type I findings.

The three trend studies addressed in the next section—TIMSS, the Progress in International Reading Literacy Study (PIRLS), and PISA—are not the only Type I studies competing for funding from the U.S. government and time in U.S. classrooms. In the past five years there have been two simultaneous cross-national surveys of technology in the classroom,[1] and in the first half of 2002 the OECD and the IEA simultaneously circulated three proposals for separate cross-national studies of teaching or teacher professional development. This proliferation of Type I studies with overlapping topics and target groups adds to the testing burden in U.S. schools, rendering it difficult to secure a valid national sample. Moreover, the limited pool of experts to design the tests and to thoughtfully consider the form of old and new measures is also strained.

The appropriate mechanism for providing such coordination for Type I studies does not currently exist. In its most expansive form, such a mechanism might be comprised of an independent advisory board broadly knowledgeable about international comparative education research, as well as the policy and practitioner communities, with separate panels for each major Type I study (playing the role of the current technical review panels) and several panels for Type II and III studies. A less ambitious mechanism would focus on Type I outcome studies only and might be a panel that is part of an existing advisory group, such as the National Assessment Governing Board or the Board on Testing and Assessment of the National Research Council. Whether board or panel, this group would serve as a peer review panel to suggest priorities, ensure

---

[1]The OECD's Information and Computer Technology study and the IEA's Second International Technology in Education Study.

that they are implemented, and help make difficult choices for the U.S. government's international comparative education research program.

Recommendation 3.1: The U.S. government should support a broadly knowledgeable body, independent of both the funders and study designers, to oversee coordination of complex and competing large-scale studies.

The immediate tasks of this body should be to oversee an impact study of TIMSS, make recommendations on TIMSS and PISA in order to avoid costly and unnecessary duplication, and review proposals for official U.S. participation in new or repeat large-scale, cross-national studies. This body should act in an anticipatory rather than a responsive way, stepping back to look at the qualities and characteristics of these studies and how they fit together, before decisions to participate. It would consider how the various studies fit together conceptually. It would identify gaps in the understanding of education in other countries; of contexts for teaching, learning, and conducting research in those countries; and of international education phenomena. Finally, this body would provide opportunities for policy makers to participate in selecting topics for an agenda and formulating research questions for future studies.

Research and Indicator Studies

The magnitude of the costs—both direct and indirect—and the need in the case of indicator studies to sustain budgetary commitments over many years make issues of duplication and coordination much more important in Type I than in Type II or III studies. In some cases, Type I research studies can, with careful planning, increase the potential return on the required investment when variables, constructs, and subgroup samples are added that expand secondary analysis opportunities. Such additions, however, carry their own costs in terms of longer questionnaires or additional survey instruments, more complex sampling frames, and increased test burden on the participants and the education systems that serve them. In the case of Type I *indicator* studies that aim to measure trends over time, the frequency with which the study is repeated and the complexity of the study framework both have the potential to increase costs. The U.S. cost of both types of studies is affected by the degree to which participating countries share the costs of the study.

Research and trend studies are not perfectly interchangeable, although sometimes they have been treated as if they are. Restructuring a research study into a trend study severely limits its usefulness as a research study. An international trend study must be carried out using very similar procedures over time and with a relatively stable group of countries. By definition, it cannot respond to changing questions and conditions without either compromising its integrity as a measure of trend or incurring the substantial additional and extraordinary costs necessary to bridge studies from old to new procedures. Methodological stasis in indicator studies is a virtue. Research studies, in contrast, are expected to build on one another, using primary and secondary analysis from one study, and from other independent studies, to advance conceptions of what associations might exist, to improve methods of measurement, and to better define important population subgroups. All of these activities involve modifying variables from one research study to the next, and the time needed to do this is usually longer than three or four years. Hence methodological stasis in research studies is a weakness, as are frequent repetitions. This suggests that the methodological imperatives of indicator studies and research studies are basically in conflict, and much is lost when research studies are also made to serve the purpose of indicator studies.

Recommendation 3.2: U.S. government sponsors should establish the purposes to be served by each component of individual studies, so that single studies will not be asked to do too much and so that expectations are clear regarding the study's potential to inform policy, produce databases appropriate for different types of primary and secondary analysis, and serve other specific functions.

In the last half of the 1990s, the United States expanded the number of Type I trend studies in which it participates from zero to three: TIMSS, PIRLS,[2] and PISA. The first of these studies, TIMSS, is implemented by an organization that had previously specialized in research studies. During the design of TIMSS 1995, IEA members pressed for additional components and variables that made the study look more like a traditional IEA research study and raised expectations that TIMSS data would be useful for a wide variety of secondary analyses. Later, others were disappointed to learn that TIMSS 1999, unlike the research studies more familiar to IEA members, would not address weaknesses recognized relatively early in TIMSS 1995, such as the need for improved assessment of common versus unique content, adjustments for between-country differences in background conditions, and analysis of within-country variance versus central tendency. As a trend study, the work on and refinement of the central

---

[2]PIRLS was first implemented by IEA in 2000 and was scheduled to be repeated in 2003; however, the schedule has changed so that it will be repeated in 2006.

variables for the TIMSS studies was essentially completed during its original design phase in 1992 and 1993 and could not be changed without disrupting the trend.

At the time TIMSS 1995 was being planned, the OECD had just begun designing PISA, and concerns about duplication were theoretical. These two studies were designed to be very different in their goals and sampling. TIMSS is intended to measure how much curricular content 4th- and 8th-grade students have learned; PISA is intended to measure the degree to which 15-year-olds can apply what they have learned in school and elsewhere to real-world situations. In practice, however, the two studies are drawing samples from one common age group in the United States and assessing common topics.

Given the lengthy time frame often necessary for the results of major education reforms in the United States to become manifest, trend studies of international student achievement probably provide valid indicators of progress no more than once or twice a decade. All the improvements expected in a research study probably cannot be addressed with only a 4-year interval between large-scale studies; at the same time, a 10-year interval is probably too long for indicator studies. PISA, with minor repeats of two skill areas and a major assessment of one area every three years, provides for a major assessment every nine years and fits in this time frame—provided it remains a relatively streamlined test, not overloaded with independent variables and components that encourage in-depth analysis of determinants of achievement better suited to a large and complex research study. In contrast, TIMSS and PIRLS are currently on four-year cycles, a frequency that may be too short for either an indicator or a research study.

Recommendation 3.3: U.S. government sponsors should avoid duplication of studies that create unnecessary costs and demand too much time from respondents.

Does the United States need to participate in three Type I trend studies in order to secure two different trends each for mathematics, science, and reading? Are they too costly? Too complicated? Too frequent? Sufficiently different in terms of their purpose and impact to justify participating in all three? More importantly, shouldn't the United States be participating in a regular Type I research study for one or more of these subjects? In addition to these questions, another is also relevant: What are the other countries participating in these studies willing to do? To date, many years of work have been invested in all these studies, and many difficult compromises have been worked out among the participating countries. These questions probably cannot be addressed by individuals and agencies deeply invested in one or more of the studies; they are better addressed by a relatively independent oversight body, such as the body described in Recommendation 3.1.

Datasets or Studies?

In our view, multiple, timely, primary and secondary analyses could play an important role in stimulating a healthy debate about the proper interpretation of Type I studies, as illustrated in the board's 1999 report on secondary analysis of TIMSS (National Research Council, 1999). The production of these analyses can be facilitated by the rapid release not simply of quantitative data and codebooks, but also of curriculum guides, student background questionnaires, videotapes, and other artifacts of the study process. Such data, properly archived, allow scholars opportunities to reanalyze the primary data as well as the artifacts that created the data. The cost of such archives, although significant, could help to maximize the return on the investment that Type I studies represent.

Nonetheless, few large-scale international studies will assemble datasets that can be used by other researchers for purposes more diverse than those underlying the original design. TIMSS, for example, was not designed to serve as a national education census for each of the participating countries. To promote appropriate use of TIMSS data, the National Science Foundation has sponsored a series of training sessions for researchers interested in analyzing the TIMSS quantitative data. The TIMSS Classroom Videotape Study has adopted a more regulatory approach: before researchers can use the video data, they must be trained and licensed.

Costs associated with collecting the data and making them available to secondary researchers need to be weighed against (1) the number of secondary researchers likely to use it, and (2) the potential impact of their work. For example, the videotapes of 8th-grade mathematics classes in the United States, Germany, and Japan have arguably generated as much interest and action as any other component of the TIMSS 1995 study: a single taped episode featuring just two classrooms in each country, one book, and related articles derived from the study have produced substantial buzz. Meanwhile, federal rules intended to protect the confidentiality of research subjects currently limit access to the TIMSS videotapes to a few licensed researchers able to travel to the TIMSS videotape study center, previously at the University of California at Los Angeles and now in Washington, D.C. Consequently, many years after the "release" of these expensive tapes, coded at significant cost, and the funding of a center to make them available to licensed researchers, no secondary research has been published.

Recommendation 3.4: U.S. government contractors and grantees should provide rapid release of quantitative data and codebooks, curriculum guides, and study artifacts from all types of studies. Federal sponsors shall assure that these materials are archived in such a way that, to the extent possible, scholars have opportunities to reanalyze primary data, and that archives are kept open and available for a decade or more.

All study designs, for all types of international studies, need to include explicit plans for both analysis and dissemination. With respect to Type I and II studies, the end-users of data need to be involved at the formulation stage of both studies and databases. For all studies, to the extent that practitioners and policy makers at the state and local levels are intended end-users, their input should be secured at the earliest stages of formulating the design and planning dissemination, and budgets should include line items for local-level analysis and dissemination of results. Doing so will necessitate more collaboration among researchers and state and local officials and practitioners than has been typical in many Type I studies to date.

Recommendation 3.5: U.S. government sponsors should set aside funding for data analysis for state and local district participants in future international benchmarking projects.

GETTING THE MOST FROM ALL STUDIES

Less than three decades ago, many Americans did not believe the U.S. education system had much to learn from countries with smaller economies and lower gross national products, such as Japan and Singapore. That is no longer the case. In recent years, both TIMSS and more general trends in globalization have increased Americans' awareness of differences in educational achievement across countries that defy economic might. However, people's understanding of the potential reasons for those differences has not necessarily increased. More Americans may be open to innovations from other countries, but the absolute number of practitioners and policy makers looking for answers to education questions in other countries remains small. Moreover, this search has been hit or miss, with misapprehension of differences in the context of education in the United States and other countries confounding attempts to experiment with and adapt techniques and curricula.

How can the portfolio of high-quality Type I, II, and III research be balanced in a way that that will both expand researchers' basic understanding of educational processes and support the efforts of practitioners, policy makers, and the public to apply this new understanding to the U.S. education system? Accomplishing this implies a more systematic approach to analysis sensitive both to the different questions each group may pose and to the complexities of communicating the results of all types of international comparative studies of education in ways appropriate to each group.

Recommendation 4: The U.S. agenda for international comparative studies in education should include a prominent place for interpretive analyses that aim to enhance public understanding of education in other countries.

> **Recommendation 4.1: Analysis plans should be developed as part of study plans so that the sampling plan, the construction and inclusion variables, and links with other datasets will support these uses.**

International comparative education studies in the United States have a long history of generating new ideas and contributing to general knowledge about education and its potential, but only occasionally have they informed national policy in an immediate, direct, and appropriate manner. As discussed in Chapter 3, the contribution of all three types of studies to efforts to improve U.S. education have been mixed, often because many have lacked mechanisms to help the public, practitioners, and policy makers make sense of and use their findings. Similarly lacking are mechanisms to help with the flow of ideas in the opposite direction, from practitioners to researchers. Practitioners continue to identify and pilot many promising internationally derived ideas, but even the most appropriate ones often founder for lack of critical information about context, such as practitioner support structures or access to extrabudgetary resources.

The TIMSS Toolkit represents one effort to disseminate artifacts and ideas—rather than arguments—from the U.S. Department of Education to practitioners at the district and local levels. Peak et al. (2002) note that one of the most popular pieces of the toolkit was a translation of a Japanese curriculum guide, something that brought to life the differences between U.S. and Japanese curriculum planning. Watching the videotapes of Japanese and German classrooms included in the kits also provided an opportunity for practitioners to raise their own questions, such as "Why don't our classrooms look like that?" Similarly, the visually engaging traveling exhibit of the Reggio Emilia approach resonated with theories already emerging in the early childhood education field in the United

States and presented an example of one way in which those theories might be translated into classroom practice.

The need for more artifacts, ideas, and results from all three types of studies tailored to practitioners, policy makers, and the public is illustrated by the relatively narrow public discourse that persists around the largest most publicized international comparative education studies, TIMSS and its follow-on studies. Despite a major public relations effort mounted by the U.S. Department of Education at the time of the TIMSS release, the majority of the public still does not understand why Japanese and Singaporean students consistently perform better on this assessment than do U.S. students. The response to poor U.S. performance has been to do more assessment and to imitate some easily accessible features of high performing countries' education systems, such as the curriculum. To the extent that practitioners and policy makers come into contact with artifacts, such as textbooks and curriculum guides, and with practitioners from other countries, and these breathe fresh air into the U.S. system, this can be a constructive process. To the extent, however, that practitioners and policy makers seize on one component of a complex foreign school system and adopt it on a large scale without first piloting it on a smaller scale and studying it in context, the results are likely to be disappointing and costly.

While Type I studies have succeeded in increasing public interest in improving U.S. schools, Type II and Type III studies hold the best hope for deepening many Americans' curiosity about education systems in the rest of the world and envisioning ways in which other ideas might enrich our own. To some foreign observers, the United States seems obsessed with the relationship between mediocre performance on TIMSS today and international economic competitiveness in the future (National Research Council, 1999:22). In contrast, some high-performing countries are looking for ways to use schooling to nurture the sort of creativity and dynamism manifest in American public life, both economic and political, and are prepared to see decreases in their scores on future international assessment to achieve that.

No specific entity in the U.S. Department of Education currently has responsibility for getting the message from Type II and III international studies out to the U.S. public. In the case of TIMSS, the National Science Foundation sponsored the work of one researcher to develop a relatively simple narrative about the TIMSS results. As noted earlier, this approach, while ensuring that at least some message gets beyond the research community, also generated a false sense of certainty about what TIMSS has to say, reducing interest in future analyses of TIMSS data. From this experience, the board concludes that communicating the results of complex Type I studies to the American public requires not a simple story line based on standard statistical analysis, but an ongoing, public discussion of the meaning and limitations of such studies and the introduction of data from other studies to inform and frame it. Different audiences find different types of data and arguments convincing and useful. Such a debate should address pivotal comparisons, such as those highlighted in Rotberg (1998). For example, what is the relative performance of the United States and high-performing countries in terms of:

- productivity in science and engineering;
- research opportunities in institutions of higher education;
- participation of women and minorities in science and engineering; and
- access to higher education in science and engineering for low-income students and historically disadvantaged groups.

Answering these kinds of questions requires more than doing another, better, large-scale survey. Rather, it requires a series of Type II and III studies to explore differences in meaningful ways that may or may not lead to operationalization of the salient variables in terms that allow quantitative comparisons.

Education researchers, whether domestic or international, have struggled to capture and maintain the attention of their intended audiences. The research and public policy communities have not invested many resources in understanding what dissemination strategies work best under what circumstances for which audiences. The idea that one story line is the best way to secure public attention, for example, has not been tested. Three Type I studies (PIRLS, PISA, TIMSS-R) that were recently released with very little fanfare provide an opportunity to experiment with various mechanisms for capturing the attention of various audiences at some time after initial release of large datasets—for example, after secondary analysis has revealed more than one new interpretation of the data. Could such differences be used to foster a healthy debate on education in the United States, or will they frustrate the public and reduce the credibility of international studies?

Recommendation 4.2: U.S. funders should support analyses from multiple perspectives as soon as possible after data have been collected so that the public can be exposed to a range of perspectives and interpretations, some complementary (addressing differing questions) and some competing (addressing similar or the same questions).

For example, the National Science Foundation has made funds available for researcher-designated secondary analysis studies of TIMSS.

Sponsoring more than one initial analysis of primary data, providing funding for secondary analysis, and investing in activities to communicate the findings of these studies to the public, however, will not foster a healthy climate of discussions by themselves. Type I studies still only answer the "what" questions, that is, "at what level are U.S. students performing?" It takes Type II and III studies to answer a higher level of question, that is, "why are U.S. students performing at this level?" and "what can be done to improve that level?" Various hypotheses about how to use different types of international studies to increase and elevate public discourse about education in the United States deserve to be explored and their impact examined.

For example, in the previous section we suggested that researchers should team up with practitioners and state and local policy makers in formulating the underlying questions for international studies, and that they return to those audiences to discuss results and dissemination in order to increase the likelihood that these audiences will make use of the results. Is that more or less effective than simply providing state and local officials and practitioners with access to more artifacts, such as videotapes and curriculum guides from other countries, and to more engaging summaries of provocative, detail-rich Type III studies? Under what circumstances? When do international components tied to domestic research studies increase the potential interest of those studies to various audiences and provide more constructive, evidence-based ways to discuss issues polarizing parts of the U.S. education community?

Recommendation 4.3: Special activities, publications, and other media should be planned to showcase the results of international studies in formats that are intelligible and engaging for practitioners, the public, and policy makers, and, when necessary, producing reports individually targeted to just one of these audiences.

In summary, the funding of multiple primary and secondary analyses and the funding for the preparation of engaging, audience-specific vehicles for communicating the results of those studies are mutually reinforcing strategies for using international studies to promote a more constructive, evidence-based discussion of ways to improve the U.S. education system.

5

Infrastructure

At the beginning of the 1990s, the international comparative education community lacked the infrastructure necessary to conduct rigorous Type I studies in a timely way. Today, thanks to work in International Assocation for the Evaluation of Educational Achievement (IEA) studies throughout the 1990s, this capacity is institutionalized in international organizations such as the International Study Center at Boston College, the IEA Data Processing Center in Hamburg, Germany, the Organisation for Economic Co-operation and Development's (OECD) Directorate for Education, and a half-dozen other nonprofit and for-profit educational research centers, such as the Australian Council for Educational Research, the Educational Testing Service in the United States, and the Japanese National Institute for Education Research. These organizations are now capable of serving most high-income and some middle-income countries. They are also now working with other organizations, such as the International Institute for Educational Planning and the Institute for Statistics of UNESCO, the World Bank, and the Inter-American Development Bank, to increase the capacity of medium- and low-income countries to gather and analyze their own education data.

At the same time, the organizations that comprise the infrastructure for Type I studies have taken on a life of their own, blurring the line between those who advocate for, who fund, and who conduct studies. This means that Type I studies have an articulate constituency, well-positioned to advocate for studies at the federal government level. Constituencies for Type II studies are relatively ad hoc, and for Type III studies constituencies are small, and generally not able to make their voices heard. The potential end-users of education research—secondary researchers, practitioners, state and local policy makers, and the public—tend to be the least well-represented constituency in federal decision making about international comparative studies. This suggests one reason why the usability of all types of education research is currently in question (Lagemann, 2002).

This chapter addresses several ways infrastructure at the federal level could increase the usability of international comparative education research by creating a more broadly participatory infrastructure to plan, conduct, and disseminate findings from all types of studies.

ORGANIZATIONAL INFRASTRUCTURE

In July 1994, the National Center for Education Statistics (NCES) drafted a "Strategic Plan for International Activities at the National Center for Education Statistics," aimed at expanding "ways to provide more information about U.S. education from an international perspective" (U.S. Department of Education, National Center for Education Statistics, 1994, 1995).[1] NCES's international activities program has since focused on developing a robust set of international education statistics, giving highest priority to the activities of cross-national collaborative data collection and analysis. Although the plan included among its main features "to emphasize the development of alternatives to large multinational education studies to collect useful comparative international data," by default its small staff has focused most of its efforts on the large studies. In the eight years since the plan was prepared, NCES has implemented it with more or less adherence to a strict interpretation of statistics, funding Type I studies and leaving the funding for more interpretive Type II and III studies to other governmental and non-governmental sponsors.

Many Type II and III studies are conducted without major funding from the federal government. Within the U.S. Department of Education, various international education directives[2] encourage learning more about effective education policies and practices in other countries, but a strategic plan for U.S. government investments encompassing Type II and III studies has not been developed.

Recommendation 5: The federal government should create a broadly participatory infrastructure to plan and conduct its international comparative education studies.

---

[1]This strategic plan for 1995-2000 was never finalized, nor were the 1995 draft considerations for implementing the strategic plan.

[2]U.S. Department of Education, Planning and Evaluation Services (2000); U.S. Department of Education (2002).

Recommendation 5.1: Although no single federal office can encompass all the responsibilities entailed in building up international comparative studies in education in the U.S. government, the U.S. Department of Education should take the lead in developing a distinct program of international comparative education research studies for the U.S. government.

The National Center for Education Statistics remains a prominent focal point for Type I studies. But with a newly reauthorized and robust Institute of Education Sciences (replacing the former Office of Educational Research and Improvement), and through the international program coordinating responsibilities of the Office of the Under Secretary, the department is clearly positioned to fulfill the leadership role for international comparative education research studies expressed in our recommendation. This program should be staffed with experts in international comparative studies in education, and its tasks should include developing policy statements to guide the agenda, inform funding decisions, and monitor all types of studies; updating existing NCES strategy for Type I studies; developing incentives for incorporating international perspectives into more domestically oriented education studies; and planning for building up the international comparative education research community.

FUNDING

The case for increasing overall funding for education research in the United States has been made in many venues and is not repeated here. Funding international comparative education research or domestic education research should not be approached as a zero-sum game, with funds for international increasing only at the expense of domestic research. Similarly, increasing funding for one type of international study should not necessarily come at the expense of another type. Results from one type of study may raise interest in and willingness to fund other types of studies; the TIMSS Videotape Classroom Study led directly to increases in funding for more qualitative or action research-oriented studies of Japanese lesson study. In addition, given relative costs, it is possible to fund scores of Type II and III studies without approaching the cost of a single repetition of a Type I study of educational achievement or literacy.

Recommendation 5.2: In efforts to create a more balanced portfolio of education research, additional funding for international comparative education studies should not be approached as a zero-sum game, with increases for international coming only at the expense

of domestic, nor with increases for Type II and III studies coming only at the expense of Type I studies.

Technology offers enormous possibilities for further data collection, yet the capacity and resources to analyze existing data lag behind; expensive, existing international comparative education databases lie underused. Assuming continued, but perhaps less frequent, Type I studies of the quality achieved in recent years, increased efforts to plan for secondary analysis at the design stage, and increased efforts to place primary and secondary data in accessible archives, the quantity of international comparative quantitative data potentially available for secondary analysis in the medium term is adequate. Except for efforts to make their findings and data more useable for various audiences and more accessible for secondary researchers, present levels of funding for Type I studies are adequate and perhaps could be reduced.

The *1993 Agenda* called for "syntheses of empirical research throughout the world, bringing such research to bear on broad comparative questions of wide interest," but almost 10 years later few such syntheses—which are most likely to qualify as Type II studies—have been undertaken. The lack of secondary analyses and cross-national syntheses of research may be attributed in part to the reward structure in the U.S. scholarly community, which values primary research more than secondary analysis and syntheses. Additional funding for the latter activities might help to shift this balance and attract a critical mass of scholars to use existing international comparative data and studies from other countries to address topics likely to become short-term policy or basic research questions in the U.S. education community.

Recommendation 5.3: Funding agencies, both governmental and nongovernmental, must take the lead in encouraging the next stage of international comparative studies, which go beyond generating high-quality education indicators and correlations, to basic education research and comparative social science.

Funding is also an issue in terms of building a field of scholars who can generate a steady and diverse flow of international comparative studies relevant to U.S. education policy. Type I studies can draw on an existing domestic pool of U.S. experts in psychometrics, statistics, and other quantitatively oriented fields. Preparation in these fields tends to be similar for both domestic and international research, and scholars in these fields do not require early specialization in international studies.

Other types of international studies, however, demand scholars who have a long-term and ongoing commitment to specialize in the education system of another culture. Such scholars must devote a substantial part of their career to developing and maintaining up-to-date language skills, area studies, cross-disciplinary skills, and institutional linkages with scholars and education systems in other countries or regions. For significant periods in their careers, these scholars may live outside the United States, and their studies may not be directly related to education. Much of the education regional expertise now extant in the United States was funded piecemeal as future scholars begin language and cultural studies through student exchange programs, proceed through Fulbright-Hays training grants, the Peace Corps, the Department of Education's foreign language and area studies fellowships, and American Association for the Advancement of Science fellowships with international development organizations, independent of funding specific to education studies. These were the scholars who were ready when U.S. policy makers and the public wanted to know why Japanese students performed so well on TIMSS.

Recommendation 5.4: Additional funding for the secondary analyses of international comparative education surveys and cross-national syntheses of important topics should be used to attract a critical mass of scholars to these relatively neglected areas. Similarly, long-term investments are needed to encourage a critical mass of education scholars to develop geographical expertise in the full range of regions, countries, and research methodologies.

All of this points to the importance of long-term investments not only to develop individual area experts, but also to develop a critical mass of scholars with specific area expertise. In the 1980s and 1990s, the work of William Cummings, Catherine Lewis, Lois Peak, Tom Rohlen, and others created a body of knowledge about Japanese education that enabled more recent scholars to make sense of new studies in far less time, with far less funding than might have been otherwise possible. Several of the scholars whose studies are cited in this report were the beneficiaries of student exchange programs and funding from the government of Japan. This enabled U.S. scholars to develop proficiency in Japanese early in their careers, leading to deeper and richer analyses later on.

Maintaining a healthy, vibrant, and diverse community of comparative education scholars involves funding for all stages of academic development. Longer-term doctoral and postdoctoral fellowships that enable U.S. scholars to develop geographical area and language specialization are relatively inexpensive long-term investments in developing the comparative international education field. In addition, establishing more linkages among U.S. school districts that are interested in implementing international innovations with the scholars who study those innovations, and exchange groups overseas also represents a modest investment in expanding the number of Americans engaged in looking for and experimenting with a broader range of innovations in education.

Japan, and perhaps other countries, have engaged more deliberately in these types of studies than has the United States. In the United States, the work of Liping Ma (Fang, 2002) is a model suggesting that tremendous dividends can be reaped from small amounts of funding to experienced teachers and senior scholars from other countries. A grant of $1,000 enabled Ma to return to China to collect her first round of data, without which she might have been unable to demonstrate to the senior scholars who later supported her work significant differences in the knowledge base of American and Chinese teachers. These dividends were increased when mentors helped Ma develop strong ties to domestically oriented departments in various U.S. schools of education, increasing the likelihood that her findings would make sense to U.S. educators. The cost of the type of study we envision might be as low as several thousand dollars. There is a large pool of foreign education students and scholars already in the United States on which to draw; facilitating their work may or may not require modest diplomatic capital; and, as noted above, the small-scale studies they undertake tend to be less demanding of student, teacher, and administrator time than Type I or II studies.

Recommendation 5.5: U.S. funders should support all stages of academic development for international comparative education scholars and encourage foreign scholars to study the U.S. education system.

6

Recommendations

In this chapter, we gather together and present the board's recommendations on three types of international comparative education studies, categorized according to their initial, primary purpose:

- Type I studies typically include large-scale surveys that aim to compare educational outcomes at various levels in two or more countries.
- Type II studies are designed to inform one or more particular U.S. education policies by studying specific topics relevant to those policies and their implementation in other countries.
- Type III studies are not designed to make direct comparisons between the United States and other countries in terms of specific policies or educational outcomes. Rather, they aim to further understanding of educational processes in different cultural and national contexts.

Recommendation 1: Funding for international comparative education research should reflect a balance among the three types of international comparative education studies and should encompass a broad array of methodologies, scales, purposes, and topics. Specifically, the United States should increase investments in studies that focus on understanding the education experiences of other countries in their own context (Type II and III), to provide a broader context for U.S. experiences and efforts to innovate (Chapter 2).

Recommendation 1.1: U.S. funders should foster closer links among practitioners and researchers so that both participate in the formulation and conduct of research, and both take responsibility for creating effective ways to use international education research.

Recommendation 1.2: U.S. funders should routinely support international components in domestic (state, local, and national) education policy and practice studies that draw on experiences in other countries.

Recommendation 1.3: U.S. funders should evaluate proposals for qualitative or historical studies and for quantitative studies by somewhat different criteria, conforming to fundamental principles of sound research for both and accommodating the different canons of systematic inquiry and different warrants for generalization in each discipline.

Recommendation 1.4: U.S. funders should encourage multicomponent research studies with longer time horizons, using a variety of qualitative and quantitative methodologies.

Recommendation 2: The United States should conduct systematic analyses of costs of the expensive Type I and II studies (including financial cost, respondent or participant burden, accommodating design shortcomings, etc.) and benefits (services received, information provided, topics studies, etc.) so that a more complete picture of impact can inform future program and funding decisions. These analyses should be "internationally comparative" in that they compare impact in the United States with impact from the same or similar studies in other countries (Chapter 3).

Recommendation 2.1: U.S. funders should move away from piecemeal, ad hoc support of international studies, and toward incorporating explicit considerations of relative cost, benefit, and impact in both the planning and the proposal review processes.

Recommendation 2.2: U.S. funders should give highest priority, of all the possible impact studies that might be undertaken, to an impact analysis of TIMSS 1995. This analysis should address TIMSS in terms of (a) its efforts to serve as both an indicator and a research study and (b) its impact on the U.S. education system.

Recommendation 2.3: U.S. funders should support reviews of the impact of different study methodologies on different audiences.

Recommendation 2.4: U.S. funders should support reviews of the impact of ongoing and completed international comparative studies on the practice of education on a planned and continuing basis to determine how effects can be enhanced.

Recommendation 3: On a continuing basis, the federal government should plan, coordinate, monitor, and modify studies in the

government's portfolio of international comparative education research (Chapter 4).

Recommendation 3.1: The U.S. government should support a broadly knowledgeable body, independent of both the funders and study designers, to oversee coordination of complex and competing large-scale studies.

Recommendation 3.2: U.S. government sponsors should establish the purposes to be served by each component of individual studies, so that single studies will not be asked to do too much and so that expectations are clear regarding the study's potential to inform policy, produce databases appropriate for different types of primary and secondary analysis, and serve other specific functions.

Recommendation 3.3: U.S. government sponsors should avoid duplication of studies that create unnecessary costs and demand too much time from respondents.

Recommendation 3.4: U.S. government contractors and grantees should provide rapid release of quantitative data and codebooks, curriculum guides, and study artifacts from all types of studies. Federal sponsors shall assure that these materials are archived in such a way that, to the extent possible, scholars have opportunities to reanalyze primary data, and that archives are kept open and available for a decade or more.

Recommendation 3.5: U.S. government sponsors should set aside funding for data analysis by state and local district participants in future international benchmarking projects.

Recommendation 4: The U.S. agenda for international comparative studies in education should include a prominent place for interpretive analyses that aim to enhance public understanding of education in other countries (Chapter 4).

Recommendation 4.1: Analysis plans should be developed as part of study plans so that the sampling plan, the construction and inclusion variables, and links with other datasets will support these uses.

Recommendation 4.2: U.S. funders should support analyses from multiple perspectives as soon as possible after data have been collected so that the public can be exposed to a range of perspectives and interpretations, some complementary (addressing differing questions) and some competing (addressing similar or the same questions).

Recommendation 4.3: Special activities, publications, and other media should be planned to showcase the results of international studies in formats that are intelligible and engaging for practitioners, the public, and policy makers, and, when necessary, producing reports individually targeted to just one of these audiences.

Recommendation 5: The federal government should create a broadly participatory infrastructure to plan and conduct its international comparative education studies (Chapter 5).

Recommendation 5.1: Although no single federal office can encompass all the responsibilities entailed in building up international comparative studies in education in the U.S. government, the U.S. Department of Education should take the lead in developing a distinct program of international comparative education research studies for the U.S. government.

Recommendation 5.2: In efforts to create a more balanced portfolio of education research, additional funding for international comparative education studies should not be approached as a zero-sum game, with increases for international coming only at the expense of domestic, nor with increases for Type II and III studies coming only at the expense of Type I studies.

Recommendation 5.3: Funding agencies, both governmental and non-governmental, must take the lead in encouraging the next stage of international comparative studies, which go beyond generating high-quality education indicators and correlations, to basic education research and comparative social science.

Recommendation 5.4: Additional funding for the secondary analyses of international comparative education surveys and cross-national syntheses of important topics should be used to attract a critical mass of scholars to these relatively neglected areas. Similarly, long-term investments are needed to encourage a critical mass of education scholars to develop geographical expertise in the full range of regions, countries, and research methodologies.

Recommendation 5.5: U.S. funders should support all stages of academic development for international comparative education scholars and encourage foreign scholars to study the U.S. education system.

References

Alexander, Robin J. (2001). *Culture and Pedagogy: International Comparisons in Primary Education*. Malden, MA: Blackwell.

Amadeo, Jo-Ann, Judith Torney-Purta, Reiner Lehmann, Vera Husfeldt, and Roumiana Nikolova (2002). *Civic Knowledge and Engagement: An IEA Study of Upper Secondary Students in Sixteen Countries*. Amsterdam: International Association for the Evaluation of Educational Achievement.

Ayalon, Hanna, and Adam Gamoran (2000). Stratification in academic secondary programs and educational inequality: Comparison of Israel and the United States. *Comparative Education Review* 44:54-80.

Berliner, David C., and Bruce J. Biddle (1995). *The Manufactured Crisis: Myths, Fraud, and the Attack on America's Public Schools*. Cambridge, MA: Perseus Books.

Black, Paul J., and J. Myron Atkin, Editors (1996). *Changing the Subject: Innovations in Science, Mathematics and Technology Education*. New York: Routledge, in association with the Organisation for Economic Co-operation and Development.

Bunt, Nancy (2001). *Southwest Pennsylvania: Using TIMSS '95 and TIMSS '99 for Local Education Reform*. Presented at TIMSS Benchmarking: Using International Data for Local Education Reform? A colloquium sponsored by the Board on Testing and Assessment and the Board on International Comparative Studies in Education, October 26, 2001. National Academy of Sciences, Washington, DC.

Chokshi, Sonal M. (2002). Impact of Lesson Study. Paper commissioned by the Board on International Comparative Studies in Education's Committee on a Framework and Long-term Research Agenda for International Comparative Education Studies. National Research Council, Washington, DC. March. Unpublished paper; to obtain a copy contact the author at smc90@columbia.edu.

Cremin, Lawrence Arthur (1990). *Popular Education and Its Discontents*. New York: Harper & Row.

Cuban, Larry (1988, January). A fundamental puzzle of school reform. *Phi Delta Kappan* 69(5):340-345.

Donmoyer, Robert (1999, October). Paradigm talk (and its absence) in the second edition of *The Handbook of Research on Educational Administration*. *Educational Administration Quarterly* 35(4):614-641.

Dossey, John A. (2002). Impact of Large-Scale Cross-National Educational Studies on Mathematics Education Standards and Curricular Efforts in the United States. Paper commissioned by the Board on International Comparative Studies in Education's Committee on a Framework and Long-term Research Agenda for International Comparative Education Studies. National Research Council, Washington, DC. March. Unpublished paper; to obtain a copy contact the author at jdossey@math.ilstu.edu.

Fang, Yanping (2002). *Impact of the Book Knowing and Teaching Mathematics by Li Ping Ma on the U.S. Mathematics Education Community*. Paper commissioned by the Board on International Comparative Studies in Education's Committee on a Framework and Long-term Research Agenda for International Comparative Education Studies. Draft. National Research Council, Washington, DC. April. Unpublished paper; to obtain a copy contact the author at fangyanp@pilot.msu.edu.

Fernandez, Clea (2002, November). Learning from Japanese approaches to professional development: The case of lesson study. *Journal of Teacher Education* 53(05).

Fiske, Edward B., and Helen F. Ladd (2000). *When Schools Compete: A Cautionary Tale*. Washington, DC: Brookings Institution.

Gamoran, Adam (1996). Curriculum standardization and equality of opportunity in Scottish secondary education, 1984-1990. *Sociology of Education* 29:1-21.

Heck, Ronald H., and Philip Hallinger (1999). Next generation methods for the study of leadership and school improvement. Chapter 7 in *Handbook of Research on Educational Administration: A Project of the American Educational Research Association*. Joseph Murphy and Karen Seashore Louis, editors. San Francisco: Jossey-Bass.

Hinckle, Pia (1991, December). A school must rest on the idea that all children are different, in Reggio Emilia: The best schools in the world. *Newsweek* 118(23):52.

Holmes, Brian. (1985). History of comparative education. *The International Encyclopedia of Education: Research and Studies, Volume 2*. Editors-in-Chief Torsten Husen and T. Neville Postlethwaite, 865-867. Oxford: Pergamon Press.

Kerckhoff, Alan C. (1986). Effects of ability grouping in British secondary schools. *American Sociological Review* 51:842-858.

Kluckhohn, Clyde (1944). *Mirror for Man: A Survey of Human Behavior and Social Attitudes*. Greenwich, CT: Fawcett.

Lagemann, Ellen Condliffe (2000). *An Elusive Science: The Troubling History of Education Research*. Chicago: University of Chicago Press.

Lagemann, Ellen Condliffe (2002). Usable Knowledge in Education. A Memorandum for the Spencer Foundation Board of Directors. January 24. The Spencer Foundation, Chicago, Illinois. Available: http://www.spencer.org/publications/usable_knowledge_report_ecl_a.htm/

Lee, Peng Yee, and Lianghuo Fan (2002). The Development of Singapore Mathematics Curriculum: Understanding the Changes in Syllabus, Textbooks and Approaches. A talk given at the Chongqing conference August 17-20, 2002. National Institute of Education, Singapore.

LeTendre, Gerald, David P. Baker, Motoko Akiba, and Alexander W. Wiseman (2001). The policy trap: National educational policy and the Third International Math and Science Study. *International Journal of Educational Policy, Research and Practice* 2(1):45-64.

LeTendre, Gerald K. (2002). Advancements in conceptualizing and analyzing cultural effects in cross-national studies of educational achievement. Pp. 198-230 in *Methodological Advances in Cross-National Surveys of Educational Achievement*. Andrew C. Porter and Adam Gamoran, editors. Board on International Comparative Studies in Education, Board on Testing and Assessment, Center for Education, Division of Behavioral and Social Sciences and Education, National Research Council. Washington, DC: National Academy Press.

Lewis, Catherine (1995a). *Educating Hearts and Minds: Reflections on Japanese Preschool and Elementary Education*. New York: Cambridge University Press.

Lewis, Catherine (1995b). The roots of Japanese educational achievement: Helping children develop bonds to school. *Educational Policy* 9(2):129-151.

Lewis, Catherine, and Ineko Tsuchida (1998). A lesson is like a swiftly flowing river: Research lessons and the improvement of Japanese education. *American Educator* Winter:12-17, 50-52.

Ma, Liping (1999). *Knowing and Teaching Elementary Mathematics: Teacher's Understanding of Fundamental Mathematics in China and the United States*. Mahwah, NJ: Lawrence Erlbaum Associates

Martin, Michael O., Keith Rust, and Raymond J. Adams, Editors (1999). *Technical Standards for IEA Studies*. Delft, The Netherlands: International Association for the Evaluation of Educational Achievement.

McEwan, Patrick J., and Martin Carnoy (2000). The effectiveness and efficiency of private schools in Chile's voucher system. *Educational Evaluation and Policy Analysis* 22(3):213-239.

Mullis, Ina V.S., Michael O. Martin, Albert E. Beaton, Eugenio J. Gonzalez, Dana L. Kelly, and Teresa A. Smith (1998). *Mathematics Achievement in Missouri and Oregon in an International Context: 1997 TIMSS Benchmarking*. Chestnut Hill, MA: Center for the Study of Testing, Evaluation, and Educational Policy, Boston College.

National Commission on Excellence in Education (1983). *A Nation at Risk: The Imperative for Educational Reform*. A Report to the Nation and the Secretary of Education, U.S. Department of Education. Washington, DC: U.S. Government Printing Office.

National Research Council (1990). *A Framework and Principles for International Comparative Studies in Education*. Board on International Comparative Studies in Education, Commission on Behavioral and Social Sciences and Education. Norman M. Bradburn and Dorothy M. Gilford, editors. Washington, DC: National Academy Press.

National Research Council (1992). *Research and Education Reform: Roles for the Office of Educational Research and Improvement*. Committee on the Federal Role in Education Research, Commission on Behavioral and Social Sciences and Education. Richard C. Atkinson and Gregg B. Jackson, editors. Washington, DC: National Academy Press.

National Research Council (1993). *A Collaborative Agenda for Improving International Comparative Studies in Education*. Board on International Comparative Studies in Education, Commission on Behavioral and Social Sciences and Education. Dorothy M. Gilford, editor. Washington, DC: National Academy Press.

National Research Council (1995). *Worldwide Education Statistics: Enhancing UNESCO's Role*. Board on International Comparative Studies in Education, Commission on Behavioral and Social Sciences and Education. James W. Guthrie and Janet S. Hansen, editors. Washington, DC: National Academy Press.

National Research Council (1997). *Taking Stock: What Have We Learned About Making Education Standards Internationally Competitive? Summary of a Workshop.* Board on International Comparative Studies in Education, Commission on Behavioral and Social Sciences and Education. Alexandra Beatty, editor. Washington, DC: National Academy Press.

National Research Council (1999). *Next Steps for TIMSS: Directions for Secondary Analysis.* Board on International Comparative Studies in Education, Board on Testing and Assessment, Commission on Behavioral and Social Sciences and Education. Alexandra Beatty, Lynn W. Paine, and Francisco O. Ramirez, editors. Washington, DC: National Academy Press.

National Research Council (2001). *The Power of Video Technology in International Comparative Research in Education.* Board on International Comparative Studies in Education, Board on Testing and Assessment, Center for Education, Division of Behavioral and Social Sciences and Education. Monica Ulewicz and Alexandra Beatty, editors. Washington, DC: National Academy Press.

National Research Council (2002a). *Methodological Advances in Cross-National Surveys of Educational Achievement.* Board on International Comparative Studies in Education, Board on Testing and Assessment, Center for Education, Division of Behavioral and Social Sciences and Education. Andrew C. Porter and Adam Gamoran, editors. Washington, DC: National Academy Press.

National Research Council (2002b). *Scientific Research in Education.* Committee on Scientific Principles for Education Research. Center for Eduction, Division of Behavioral and Social Sciences and Education. Richard J. Shavelson and Lisa Towne, editors. Washington, DC: National Academy Press.

New, Rebecca S. (2002). The Impact of the Reggio Emilia Model on Early Childhood Education in the U.S. Paper commissioned by the Board on International Comparative Studies in Education's Committee on a Framework and Long-term Research Agenda for International Comparative Education Studies. National Research Council, Washington, DC. Draft. July. Unpublished paper; to obtain a copy contact the author at becky.new@tufts.edu.

Organisation for Economic Co-operation and Development (1999). *Measuring Student Knowledge and Skills: A New Framework for Assessment.* Paris: OECD.

Organisation for Economic Co-operation and Development (2001). *Knowledge and Skills for Life: First Results from PISA 2000.* Paris: OECD.

Peak, Lois (2002). How the U.S. Adopts Educational Methods from Other Countries. Presentation at American Educational Research Association Annual Meeting. April 1. New Orleans.

Peak, Lois, Pat O'Connell Ross, and Jill Edwards Staton (2002). Bridging the Gap Between International Research and Educational Practice: A Case Study of the U.S. Department of Education TIMSS Resource Kit. Paper prepared for the Board on International Comparative Studies in Education's Committee on a Framework and Long-term Research Agenda for International Comparative Education Studies. National Research Council, Washington, DC. Draft. April. Unpublished paper; to obtain a copy contact the authors at lois.peak@ed.gov.

Plank, David N. (2002). The Domestic Policy Impact of International Evidence: The Case of School Choice. Paper commissioned by the Board on International Comparative Studies in Education's Committee on a Framework and Long-term Research Agenda for International Comparative Education Studies. National Research Council, Washington, D.C. April. Unpublished paper; to obtain a copy contact the author at dnplank@msu.edu.

Postlewhwaite, T. Neville (1967). *School Organization and Student Achievement: A Study Based on Achievement in Mathematics in Twelve Countries.* Stockholm: Almqvist and Wiksell.

Postlethwaite, T. Neville. (1999). *International Studies of Educational Achievement: Methodological Issues.* Hong Kong: Comparative Education Research Centre, University of Hong Kong.

Raizen, Senta A. (2002). From Rhetoric to the Classroom: The Impact of TIMSS on Science Education in the U.S. Paper commissioned by the Board on International Comparative Studies in Education's Committee on a Framework and Long-term Research Agenda for International Comparative Education Studies. National Research Council, Washington, DC. March. Unpublished paper; to obtain a copy contact the author at sraizen@wested.org.

Raizen, Senta A., and Edward D. Britton, Editors (1997). *Bold Ventures: Patterns Among Innovations in Science and Mathematics Education.* Dordrecht: Kluwer Academic.

Rotberg, Iris C. (1998, May). Interpretation of international test score comparisons. *Science* 280:1030-1031.

Rothman, Robert (2002). The Impact of International Studies in Education: The View of Education Journalists. Paper commissioned by the Board on International Comparative Studies in Education's Committee on a Framework and Long-term Research Agenda for International Comparative Education Studies. National Reseach Council, Washington, DC. March. Unpublished paper; to obtain a copy contact the author at Robert_rothman@brown.edu.

Rust, Val D., Aminata Soumaré, Octavio Pescador, and Magumi Shibnya (1999, February). Research strategies in comparative education *Comparative Education Review* 43(1):86-109.

Schmidt, William, Curtis McKnight, and Senta Raizen (1997). *A Splintered Vision: An Investigation of U.S. Science and Mathematics Education.* Boston: Kluwer Academic Publishers.

Schmidt, William H., Curtis McKnight, Gilbert A. Valverde, Richard T. Houang, and David E. Wiley (1997). *Many Visions, Many Aims. Volume 1: A Cross-National Investigation of Curricular Intentions in School Mathematics.* Dordrecht, The Netherlands: Kluwer Academic.

Schmidt, William H., Senta A. Raizen, Edward D. Britton, Leonard J. Bianchi, and Richard G. Wolfe (1997). *Many Visions, Many Aims. Volume 2: A Cross-National Investigation of Curricular Intentions in School Science.* Dordrecht, The Netherlands: Kluwer Academic.

Steiner-Khamsi, Gita, Judith Torney-Purta, and John Schwille (2002). *New Paradigms and Recurring Paradoxes in Education for Citizenship.* Boston: JAI.

Stevenson, Harold W., and James W. Stigler (1992). *The Learning Gap: Why Our Schools Are Failing and What We Can Learn from Japanese and Chinese Education.* New York: Simon and Schuster.

Stigler, James W., and James Hiebert (1999). *The Teaching Gap: Best Ideas from the World's Teachers for Improving Education in the Classroom.* New York: Simon and Schuster.

Torney-Purta, Judith, John Schwille, and Jo-Ann Amadeo (1999). *Civic Education Across Countries: Twenty-Four National Case Studies from the IEA Civic Education Project.* Amsterdam: International Association for the Evaluation of Educational Achievement.

Torney-Purta, Judith, Reiner Lehman, Hans Oswald, and Wolfram Schultz (2001). *Citizenship and Education in Twenty-Eight Countries: Civic Knowledge and Engagement at Age Fourteen.* Amsterdam: International Association for the Evaluation of Educational Achievement.

United Nations Children's Fund (2002). *A League Table of Educational Disadvantage in Rich Nations.* Innocenti Report Card. Issue No. 4, November. Florence, Italy: UNICEF Innocenti Research Centre. Available: http://www.unicef-icde.org

U.S. Congress (2002). Education Sciences Reform Act of 2002: To provide for improvement of Federal education research, statistics, evaluation, information, and dissemination, and for other purposes. (PL 107-279 Stat. 1940) HR3801.

U.S. Department of Education (2002). *Paige Outlines New International Education Priorities: Announces Plans to Bolster Education Partnerships, Honor Teachers Who Contribute to International Education Efforts.* Press release, November 20. Washington, DC: U.S. Department of Education. Available: http://www.ed.gov/pressreleases.

U.S. Department of Education, National Center for Education Statistics (1985). *Report of the International Education Statistics Conference.* Washington, DC: U.S. Department of Education.

U.S. Department of Education, National Center for Education Statistics (1994). *Strategic Plan for International Activities at the National Center for Education Statistics.* Jeanne E. Griffith, Eugene H. Owen, and David P. Baker. Washington, DC: U.S. Department of Education.

U.S. Department of Education, National Center for Education Statistics (1995). Considerations for Implementing the Strategic Plan for 1995-2000. Dorothy M. Gilford. Draft., U.S. Department of Education, National Center for Education Statistics, Washington, DC.

U.S. Department of Education, National Educational Research Policy and Priorities Board (2001). *Investing in Learning: A Policy Statement with Recommendations on Research in Education. Investing in Research: A Second Policy Statement with Further Recommendations for Research in Education.* Washington, DC: U.S. Department of Education.

U.S. Department of Education, Office of Educational Research and Improvement (1997). *Attaining Excellence: A TIMSS Resource Kit.* Washington, DC: U.S. Department of Education.

U.S. Department of Education, Office of Educational Research and Improvement (1998). *The Educational System in Japan: Case Study Findings.* Washington, DC: U.S. Department of Education.

U.S. Department of Education, Office of Educational Research and Improvement (1999). *The Educational System in Germany: Case Study Findings.* Washington, DC: U.S. Department of Education.

U.S. Department of Education, Planning and Evaluation Services (2000). Strengthening the U.S. Government's Leadership in Promoting International Education: A Discussion Paper. November 15. Available: http://www.ed.gov/officesous/pes/discussion_paper.html

U.S. Department of Education, Planning and Evaluation Services (2002). Evaluation of the Introduction of the Singapore Mathematics Approach in U.S. Schools: Statement of Work. EEA 010009. Washington, DC: U.S. Department of Education.

Weick, Karl E. (1976, March). Educational organizations as loosely coupled systems. *Administrative Science Quarterly* 21:1-19.

Weiss, Carol Hirschon (1991). Policy research: Data, ideas, or arguments? Pp. 307-332 in *Social Sciences and Modern States: National Experiences and Theoretical Crossroads.* Peter Wagner, Carol Hirschon Weiss, Bjvrn Wittrock, and Hellmut Wollmann, editors. New York: Cambridge University Press.

Weiss, Carol Hirschon (1998). *Evaluation: Methods for Studying Programs and Policies.* Upper Saddle River, NJ: Prentice Hall.

Wineburg, Sam (1997a, Autumn). Beyond "breadth and depth": Subject matter knowledge and assessment. *Theory Into Practice* 97(4):255-272.

Wineburg, Sam (1997b, September). T.S. Eliot, collaboration, and the quandaries of assessment in a rapidly changing world. *Phi Delta Kappan* 79(1):59-66.

Wiseman, Alexander W., and David P. Baker (2002). A Preliminary Report on the Impact of TIMSS-Related Activities on U.S. Education, 1996-2000. Paper commissioned by the Board on International Comparative Studies in Education's Committee on a Framework and Long-term Research Agenda for International Comparative Education Studies. Draft. National Research Council, Washington, DC. April. Unpublished paper; to obtain a copy contact the authors at alex-wiseman@utulsa.edu.

Yoshida, Makoto (1999). Lesson Study: A Case Study of a Japanese Approach to Improving Instruction Through School-based Teacher Development. Doctoral dissertation, University of Chicago.

Biographical Sketches

EMERSON J. ELLIOTT (*Chair*) is director of the Program Standards and Evaluation Project at the National Council for Accreditation of Teacher Education. He is also an independent consultant to the Indiana University's National Survey of Student Engagement and to the National Center for Public Policy and Higher Education's indicators project. He served as the first commissioner of education statistics in the U.S. Department of Education and has consulted with the Department's National Educational Research Policy and Priorities Board. He was elected an American Statistical Association fellow and has received presidential rank awards for meritorious and distinguished executive service. His service with the National Research Council includes membership on the Committee on Strategic Education Research Program Feasibility Study. Elliott has an M.A. in public administration from the University of Michigan.

DAVID C. BERLINER is Regents' professor of educational leadership and policy studies and professor of psychology in education and former dean of the College of Education at Arizona State University. His research has focused on the study of teaching, teacher education, and educational policy. He has taught at the University of Massachusetts, the University of Arizona, and at universities abroad. His publications include *Educational Psychology* and *The Manufactured Crisis*. Among his many awards are the friend of education award from the National Education Association, the distinguished contributions award of the American Educational Research Association, and the E.L. Thorndike Award of the Division of Educational Psychology of the American Psychological Association. He has served as president of the American Educational Research Association and the American Psychological Association, and as a member of the National Research Council's Board on Testing and Assessment. He has a Ph.D. in educational psychology from Stanford University.

COLETTE CHABBOTT is the director of the Board on International Comparative Studies in Education. Prior to joining the National Research Council in 2000, she served for three years as director of the masters' program in international comparative education at Stanford University. She has been working for more than 20 years on staff and as a consultant for international development organizations, including the U.S. Agency for International Development, the Rockefeller Foundation, CARE, and the Bangladesh Rural Advancement Committee, specializing in education for the past 10 years. She is the author of *Constructing Education for Development: International Organizations and "Education for All"* (2002). She has a B.A. in economics from the University of North Carolina at Chapel Hill, an M.P.A. in development policy from Princeton University, and an A.M. in sociology and a Ph.D. in education from Stanford University.

CLEA FERNANDEZ is an assistant professor of psychology and education in the Department of Human Development at Columbia University Teachers College. Her research interests are in the analysis of classroom processes with a special emphasis on cross-cultural comparisons, the psychology of learning from instruction, and teachers' theories of instruction and teacher development. She has served as director of programs and research with Classroom, Inc., helping state school systems to implement computer-based simulations for use by teachers and students. She also served as codirector of the videotape case studies project of the Third International Mathematics and Science Study, and has coauthored several journal articles and book chapters on Japanese and American mathematics education. She has a Ph.D. from the University of Chicago.

ADAM GAMORAN is a professor of sociology and educational policy studies at the University of Wisconsin, Madison. His research focuses on stratification and resource allocation in school systems. While a Fulbright fellow at the University of Edinburgh, he studied curriculum change and educational inequality in Scotland. Along with Andrew C. Porter, he served as co-editor of *Methodological Advances in Cross-National Surveys of Educational Achievement*, a recent National Research Council report by the Board on International Comparative Studies in Education. Other publications focus on student achievement, curriculum, and organizational analysis in education. He has a Ph.D. in education from the University of Chicago.

LARRY V. HEDGES is Stella M. Rowley professor at the University of Chicago in the Departments of Education, Psychology, and Sociology. He has authored and coauthored numerous books and articles on statistical methods for research and is editor of the *Journal of Educational and Behavioral Statistics*. He is a fellow of the American Statistical Association, a fellow of the American Psychological Association, and recipient of the review of research award from the American Educational Research Association. His National Research Council service includes membership on the Committee on the Evaluation of National and State Assessments of Educational Progress, the Forum on Educational Excellence and Testing Equity, and the Panel on the Combination of Information. Hedges has a Ph.D. in mathematical methods in educational research from Stanford University.

HENRY W. HEIKKINEN is a professor emeritus of chemistry at the University of Northern Colorado, specializing in chemical education. His current interests focus on curriculum development in general chemistry, student preconceptions, and implications of standards-based education reforms in science. He has served as a member of the U.S. Steering Committee for the Third International Mathematics and Science Study. He has also served as a consultant to the American Association for the Advancement of Science Project 2061 and as a chemistry education consultant in numerous countries. His National Research Council service includes membership on the Commission on Life Sciences and the Content Working Group of the National Science Education Standards. Heikkinen has a Ph.D. in chemical education from the University of Maryland.

JEREMY KILPATRICK is Regents professor at the University of Georgia Department of Mathematics Education. He has served on advisory boards of the Project on Science, the Mathematics and Technology Education in OECD Countries and the Core-Plus Mathematics Project. He has also served on national and international committees for the Trends in International Mathematics and Science Study (TIMSS 1995, 1999, and 2003); as a U.S. representative to the Programme for International Student Assessment (PISA) Mathematics Forum; and as a researcher for the Mathematics Case Studies of U.S. Innovations in Science and Technology Education. His National Research Council service includes membership on the Mathematical Sciences Education Board and the Mathematics Learning Study Committee (as chair). He has a Ph.D. in mathematics education from Stanford University.

SHARON LEWIS is director of research for the Council of the Great City Schools, where she is responsible for developing and maintaining a research program that articulates the status, needs, attributes, operation, and challenges of urban public schools and their students. She previously served in the Detroit Public Schools as assistant superintendent for the Department of Research, Development, and Coordination, and as director of the Office of Research, Evaluation, and Testing. She has also served as an international educational consultant to the U.S. Department of Defense Dependents Schools and as a State of Michigan delegate to the Soviet Union and the People's Republic of China. Her National Research Council Service has included membership on the committees on Next Steps in Educational Research, Practice, and Progress; Evaluation of National and State Assessments of Educational Progress; and Appropriate Uses of Educational Testing. Lewis has an M.A. degree in educational research from Wayne State University.

LYNN W. PAINE is an associate professor in the Department of Teacher Education at Michigan State University. Her research interests focus on understanding teaching and teacher education as contextualized practices. She currently serves as codirector of a study of mathematics and science new teacher induction in selected countries. She has also served as a researcher with a Spencer Foundation cross-national study of teacher education and as a board member of the Comparative and International Education Society. Her publications include chapters in *The Political Dimension of Teacher Education* and *Oxford Studies in Comparative Education*. She has also served as a member of the National Research Council Committee on Continuing to Learn from TIMSS. Paine has a Ph.D. in international development from Stanford University.

JANET WARD SCHOFIELD is a professor of psychology and a senior scientist at the Learning Research and Development Center at the University of Pittsburgh. Her research interests focus on the impact of social and technological change on classroom processes. She has served as a consultant to the U.S. Office of Technology Assessment and to the associate commissioner for equal educational opportunity at the U.S. Department of Education, as well as to state government bodies and local school districts. Her numerous publications include three books: *Classroom Culture, Black and White in School: Trust, Tension or Tolerance?*, and *Bringing the Internet to School: Lessons from an Urban District*. She is a fellow of the American Psychological Association and the American Psychological Society. She has a Ph.D. in social psychology from Harvard University.

JOSEPH TOBIN is a professor in the College of Education at Arizona State University. Previously he was a professor in the College of Education at the University of Hawaii and a visiting professor in human development at the University of Chicago. His research interests include educational ethnography, Japanese culture and education, visual anthropology, early childhood education, and children and the media. His publications include *Preschool in Three Cultures* and others on early childhood education and classroom ethnography. He has a Ph.D. in human development from The University of Chicago.

MONICA ULEWICZ is a program officer for the Board on International Comparative Studies in Education. Her primary responsibilities with the board have been related to its work on methodological advances in cross-national surveys of educational achievement and video technology. She co-edited the Board's report entitled *The Power of Video Technology in International Comparative Research in Education*. Her professional experience includes teacher professional development and evaluation of programs with the Eisenhower Regional Consortium for Mathematics and Science Education at AEL, Inc. She served as a Peace Corps volunteer in Uganda, managing a conservation education program funded jointly by the U.S. Agency for International Development and the Wildlife Conservation Society. She has a masters of environmental management from Duke University and a B.A. in biology, with college honors, from Earlham College.